Responsive
EVALUATION

*Making valid
judgments
about
student
literacy*

*Edited by
Brian Cambourne
and
Jan Turbill*

Heinemann
Portsmouth, NH

First published in 1994

Heinemann
A division of Reed Elsevier Inc.
361 Hanover Street
Portsmouth, NH 03801-3912

Offices and agents throughout the world

Published simultaneously in the United States
in 1994 by Heinemann
and in Australia by
Eleanor Curtain Publishing
906 Malvern Road
Armadale, Australia 3143

Library of Congress Cataloging-in-Publication Data

Responsive evaluation: making valid judgments about students' literacy/
Brian Cambourne and Jan Turbill, editors.

    p.   cm
    Includes bibliographical references.
    ISBN 0-435-08829-7

    1. Educational tests and measurements – Australia. 2. Language arts
(Elementary) – Australia – Ability testing. 3. Literacy – Australia – Evaluation.
I. Cambourne, Brian. II. Turbill, Jan.
LB3058. A8R47   1994   94-29683
372.6' 044-dc20   CIP

Contents

Preface

The thinking inherent in this book began way back somewhere around 1986. In subsequent years many teachers, students and their parents in Australia, America and Canada have been involved in some way and thus continued to challenge us and fuel our thinking. It is impossible to know just how many, but it is critical that their contributions be acknowledged.

The team — better known as 'the troops' — who have contributed to this book has been part of a large research project for several years. They came together to present a Preconference Institute at the International Reading Association in San Antonio, USA, in 1993. It was indeed an exciting and stimulating experience for the ten 'Aussies from Down Under'. After much preparation and nervous energy, the day went well. We were on a high when Eleanor Curtain invited us to pull all the presentations together and write a book. We quickly and gladly accepted. After all, we believe the hard part was done. We had prepared our work and presented it to 150 people at IRA; writing a book would be easy!

We all soon discovered writing for a different audience and purpose does make a difference in the writing. After many meetings and much prodding from our editors a manuscript finally appeared. It has been a wonderful collaborative learning experience for us all.

We must thank Jan Hancock who worked so hard with us in the project but did not quite make it to IRA. We also wish to thank the South Coast Region Department of School Education for their faith in our work and their constant support. Dr Terry Burke, Bryan Cowling and Fred Cook are leaders who are 'committed to putting teachers in charge in their teaching'. This book is an outcome of such a commitment to teachers. Student learning outcomes can only benefit as a result.

Finally to all those children who constantly challenged and informed us as learners we thank you. This book is for you.

Brian Cambourne & Jan Turbill

Introduction

'I keep gathering all this stuff on the kids But I don't quite know what it tells me.' (Grade 4 teacher, 1992)

'It's all in my head and I know I've got to make it all visible to myself, the parents and the kids. But how?' (Kindergarten teacher, 1993)

'Observation is the big thing — I observe my kids but there seems to be so much going on I don't know what I'm looking for.' (Grade 6 teacher, 1992)

'I take hours to write reports for kids but parents still say, "But where does my child rank in the class?"' (Grade 4/5 composite teacher, 1991)

'Are the standardised tests really that bad? We have to give our kids at least one don't we?' (Principal, 1993)

'Are the judgements I make too subjective? I've read lots of the new books around, but I still worry is it all too subjective? Are my findings and judgements valid? Or should I check it out with a test?' (Grade 3 teacher, 1992)

'Are teachers truly capable of making valid judgements about student achievement of educational outcomes? Do external measures provide more reliable data, more readily aggregated to provide systemic information? Can all stakeholders in a child's education be assured that evaluation in the hands of teachers is rigorous, valid and authentic?' (Cluster director, 1993)

Familiar comments and/or questions in the staff room? At staff meetings? At principals' meetings? Evaluating children's learning seems to have become a dominant concern in the educational community over the last few years, and this is especially true in the area of literacy learning. This book tells the 'story' of the journey that a group of educators, which included classroom teachers, school principals, cluster/regional directors and university researchers, took to address some of the issues involved.

Although each member of this group was intimately involved in education, in the day-to-day ebb and flow of their professional lives they had to deal with distinctly different assessment and evaluation issues. The classroom teachers, for example, had to confront and resolve assessment/evaluation issues which were different from those faced by the school principals, which in turn were different from those of cluster directors and university researchers.

Despite this, each group member had two things in common:
• a strong commitment to optimal literacy learning for all students

- a developing sense of uneasiness with traditional methods of evaluation that they were expected to employ

It was these common points of view that drew them together to address the concerns they had about the issue of evaluating children's literacy learning.

WHAT WERE THESE CONCERNS?

One common concern was a marked lack of congruence between the way they thought literacy should be *taught*, and the way they were expected to *assess* it.

Another was a strong sense of discomfort with the assessment and evaluation instruments that seemed to dominate the profession. They had become increasingly suspicious of assessment instruments such as comprehension passages with multiple choice and 'pick the mistake' type questions, or artificially constructed cloze and/or maze passages. They were not convinced that such methods were capable of demonstrating all that learners knew, understood or did, in the name of reading, writing, spelling and other accoutrements of effective literacy. They believed that these instruments were basically invalid for the job they were supposed to do; namely, to accurately reflect the degree to which students had control over the literacy practices that were used in the real world. For example, they found it difficult to accept that reading skills and other know-how, such as the ability to 'read between the lines' in order to identify the possible agendas of those who originally constructed the texts, could be evaluated using such instruments. They were also concerned that such tests included culturally specific factors that created barriers to learners in culturally diverse classrooms.

They also felt a strong concern about social equity and the use of traditional approaches to assessment. In particular, they were concerned that reducing learners' efforts to a score, a grade or a band level did not truly represent the richness of the learning experiences that their students experienced. This concern was related to parents' demands for measurement-based indicators of success, such as place in class, subject grades and percentages. They were convinced that such demands were a consequence of a lack of awareness about alternative methods of reporting information about student learning .

At about the same time, an Australia-wide interest in outcomes-based education began to emerge, and it was enthusiastically embraced by policy makers in most states. A national English profile was developed by the federal government and the NSW Department of School Education adopted an outcomes-based approach to its new English K–6 syllabus. This document defines 'outcomes' as 'the demonstrable learning achievements in English' and states that the syllabus is based on 'an outcomes standards framework'. (English K–6 syllabus 1994, p. 11) The NSW syllabus has drawn on the national English profile in that language learning and development is described in levels of achievement. These levels are to be seen as benchmarks or standards to which students' achievements could be compared, regardless of age or grade.

All these concerns were compounded in 1988 when the NSW state government introduced mass testing of literacy and numeracy for grades 6 and 3 (the Basic Skills Testing Program).

Each member of our team was unanimous on the possible confusion that such innovations could cause among teachers who had to implement and accommodate such dramatic changes. They felt the need to understand more deeply the theories behind the whole area of assessment and evaluation. They did not wish to subvert or deny the use of mandatory tests of basic skills, but wanted to understand how to use them in a curriculum designed around an 'outcomes standards framework' model to support student learning, rather than allowing them to become a straightjacket into which children's learning was inexorably squeezed.

They believed that one way of countering the possible toxic effects of such rapid change would be to develop, implement, and articulate alternative forms of assessment and evaluation. They were also convinced of the need to convince parents and the general public that there were assessment and evaluation alternatives that were authentic, credible and reliable, and which could support both the basic skills tests and the move towards an outcomes standards framework of curriculum, which included achievement profiles as guides for evaluating learning. They realised that new attitudes towards the practices of evaluating and reporting student learning outcomes needed to be fostered.

Therefore, they decided to collaborate in a research project to address these concerns.

THE PROJECT

The personnel in the project were:
- 30 self-nominated teachers from seven schools, some of whom had been co-researching this assessment and evaluation issue for a number of years
- two principals
- a curriculum consultant
- a cluster director
- four teacher educators from two separate universities

The research process employed was teacher-as-co-researcher (TACOR). This methodology involves all the co-researchers in personal and collaborative reflection, discussion, planning, sharing and refining of ideas and practices for collecting and analysing information about student learning. Those who were not classroom teachers (the teacher educators, the principals, the curriculum adviser and the cluster director) co-researched with 4–5 teachers at each of the seven schools. The classroom was the unit of research.

The basic research question had three prongs:
- Is there a model of evaluation which would meet our needs and address our concerns?
- Is it possible to apply the axioms and practices of such a model to the classroom context?
- How can this be done?

Each group of participants collected data from their classroom 'sites' (at least weekly), met weekly or bi-weekly, and regularly provided each other with peer support. The sense of working as a team and joint ownership of outcomes were clearly evident at these meetings which also provided opportunities for reflection on the achievements and direction of the project.

DEVELOPING SHARED MEANINGS

As the members of the project came from such diverse backgrounds, we found that in the early stages we needed to meet in order to develop what we called 'shared meanings', especially of the terms *assessment* and *evaluation*. This was necessary because there were some quite different definitions being used in the field at the time. For example, the NSW Department of School Education officially defined 'assessment' as pertaining to student learning, and 'evaluation' as pertaining to programs of learning. (English K–6 Syllabus pp. 82–4) This definition implied that 'assessment' related to the collection, analysis and interpretation of information associated with children's learning, whereas 'evaluation' referred to the collection, analysis, and interpretation of information associated with the merit and worth of the programs of instruction which teachers designed and implemented.

On the other hand, there were many who defined 'assessment' as the act of collecting information, whereas 'evaluation' was the act of passing judgement on or 'putting a value on' that information. We also found that at the beginning of the project some of us used the terms interchangeably and synonymously, while others argued that one (evaluation) contained or included the other (assessment) and so used only the term 'evaluation' .

After much discussion we agreed that **assessment** was 'the gathering of data' and **evaluation** was 'the making of value judgements on these data' irrespective of whether the data referred to students or teaching programs. We also recognised that the concepts represented by these two terms were interdependent, that is, the better the data we collected (assessment) the better our judgements (evaluation) could be. If we collected shoddy or faulty information then the resultant evaluation would also be shoddy and faulty. In other words, *Garbage in means garbage out.*

In the following chapters, the journey that these educators took to deal with these concerns is told in more detail. Chapter 1 describes some of the history behind changing ideologies of and beliefs about evaluation, and traces the movement from traditional measurement-based evaluation to more qualitative forms. Chapter 2 introduces the the concepts associated with one such qualitative form, namely **responsive evaluation**. Chapter 3 describes the broad findings of the research which are expanded and elaborated in the remaining chapters. Chapters 4, 5, 6, 7, 8 describe in detail how teachers implemented the findings that emerged from this research. Chapters 9 and 10 describe how two principals went about changing the assessment and evaluation cultures of their schools, and Chapter 11 gives a system-wide perspective from a cluster director. The final chapter deals with the vexed issues of validity, objectivity, and reliability, and describes how to ensure the charge that responsive evaluation is soft, non-rigorous and subjective can be refuted.

1

Why is evaluation of learning such a 'hot' issue?

What's the problem?

by Brian Cambourne

These are good questions. When we began this project we were aware that there were differences of opinion about the purposes for and methods of evaluating student learning. At one extreme, there were those who believed that the major purposes for evaluating student learning was to rank learners and compare them in terms of achievement in order to hold both teachers and learners accountable. At the other extreme, there were those who believed that evaluation should never be comparative, should never serve as a mechanism for either letting students into, or keeping them out of, some program, class, or faculty. In between these extremes there was a wide diversity of other strongly held beliefs.

There were those who strongly believed that only tests with standardised procedures of administration and interpretation were accurate, fair and valid indicators of learning. Advocates of this opinion argued that objectivity was an essential requirement of any evaluative procedure, and that quantitative measurement with standardised instruments was the only way to be certain of achieving this. There was also a growing band of adversaries of this position who had begun to question many of the assumptions about the accuracy, objectivity, validity and fairness behind measurement-based evaluation. They argued strongly that it was not possible to construct instruments that could measure something as complex as learning to be literate in ways that could ever be accurate or fair or objective, and at the same time validly reflect all that a learner knew or could do. These positions were strongly entrenched. Both advocates and adversaries were prepared to defend their own points of view with vigor.

Because there was a great deal of debate at a number levels within and outside the profession, we felt a need to understand the views from all sides. We were convinced that if we were to justify a position that was going to be helpful and useful to teachers and learners, we had to come to that position from an informed base.

CONFLICTING VIEWS OF ASSESSMENT AND EVALUATION

It seemed that those who held widely divergent views did so because they tended to view the world and interpret what they saw and heard differently. It was as if they filtered this information through different frameworks or lenses which influenced their interpretation.

Many of us first became aware of this phenomenon during the writing revolution that occurred in the 1980s. For example, one of our co-researchers described something that many of us had experienced in the early days of this revolution. She described how she sent a child home with the piece of writing shown in Figure 1.1.

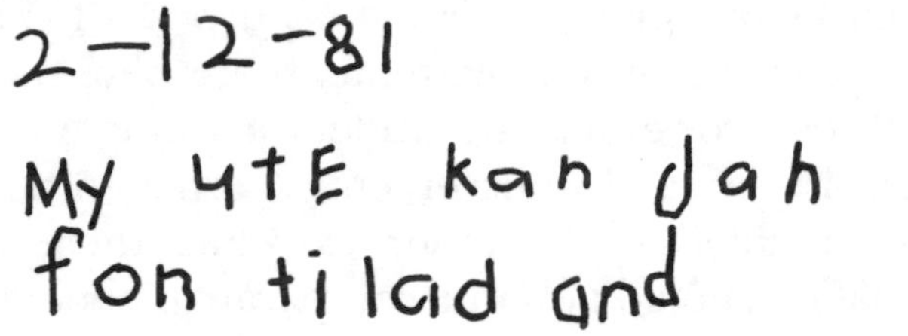

2-12-81

My 4tE kan dah
fon ti lad and
She ba bot me
and my bhother
Sun little ka s
and She Pot
Sun nahl POIE lt
Me weh I
WEt lh the
Pll it kan of.
kan

Figure 1.1: My auntie came down from Thailand and she bought me and my brother some little cubes and she put some nail polish on me. When I went in the pool it came off.

She explained how she saw the piece as a brilliant example of a very young child exploring the phonemic system of the language and drawing on her underdeveloped control of the written form of the language to construct new knowledge and skills. She believed the logic and reasoning behind some of the child's unconventional spellings to be brilliant examples of a burgeoning linguistic intelligence that suggested that this learner was well on the way to acquiring literacy. There were many indicators that demonstrated to her that this student was achieving many of the desired outcomes of English teaching.

She went on to explain how crushed she was when an angry parent called at the school the next day with an obviously chastened child, and began to wave the piece under her nose, demanding to know why such shoddy work had been tolerated or even encouraged, and threatening to report her to the principal if she didn't begin to teach her child correctly. The parent complained that *the spelling hasn't been corrected and the handwriting not even checked*.

Here were two people looking at the same piece of writing and interpreting it in diametrically opposite ways. Each had a completely different set of values, beliefs, understandings, experiences and ways of thinking about what 'effective' or 'good' writing was. All these things had come together in each of their minds to create a framework or set of lenses that forced them to view the same piece of writing in quite different ways.

THE CONCEPT OF 'PARADIGM'

Such a framework for organising and interpreting what we see and hear is called a **paradigm**. We also learned that:

- paradigms are made up of the sum total of commonly held beliefs, values, concepts, and ways of thinking about and solving problems that a community or groups within a community hold at any one time;
- paradigms influence they way that we construct reality: that is, how we interpret and understand the world;
- the ways that humans think about most areas of knowledge are framed by, perhaps even controlled by, the prevailing or most widely held paradigm of the time;
- paradigms can wax and wane in favor. When enough members of a culture or community accept a paradigm it becomes the prevailing one which determines the way that a community (or culture within that community) identifies and resolves problems;
- prevailing paradigms are continually being challenged and often begin to lose their favored status. When this occurs it is referred to as a **paradigm shift**;

- those who are wedded to a prevailing paradigm that begins to be challenged by an emerging one often fight hard to retain the status quo. Often they refuse to recognise that there could be some value in the emerging paradigm. Such groups are sometimes described as being in a state of **paradigm paralysis**;
- if the group suffering paradigm paralysis is vocal enough, they in turn begin to challenge and discredit the new paradigm, arguing strongly for a return to the status quo. Sometimes they succeed. More often they manage to modify some of the new paradigm's practices. When this happens it is called **paradigm regression**.

A familiar example of paradigm, paradigm shift, paradigm paralysis and paradigm regression relates to the environment. In the 1940s and 50s, the prevailing paradigm was that it was OK to throw rubbish into the scrubland and swamps. It was seen by many as landfill. Pouring sewage and toxic wastes into rivers and oceans seemed to be a practical thing to do. No one seemed to understand that water systems were being dangerously polluted, or that thousands of animal and plant species were becoming extinct. We were encouraged to be a society of waste-makers, behaving as if the earth's resources were infinite; we were encouraged to buy, use, throw away, and then buy some more. The concept of recycling was neither valued nor practised. Economic growth and the development of wealth were the driving set of beliefs behind this paradigm and there was little research directed at understanding the ramifications of such behavior.

However, little by little our knowledge grew as scientists and conservationists researched these areas. The more society came to know and understand, the more pressure for change was brought to bear. The paradigm began to shift.

We are all now aware that the paradigm *has* shifted. The conservation movement and a new breed of scientists have seriously challenged the old attitudes and we are now prepared to go the trouble of sorting our household garbage so that it can be recycled. Goods that are made from recycled materials have high status in the commercial world and the recycling industry is becoming an important part of our economy. The sum total of commonly held beliefs, values, concepts, and ways of thinking about and solving problems of the environment that our community currently holds has changed, and most of us could never go back.

There are, however, some of us who are sometimes unwittingly, sometimes quite consciously, in paradigm paralysis. Many of us have elderly parents who simply can't understand the recycling of garbage practice and who continue to put all their garbage in the one trash can, and are surprised when the garbage collector won't take it. Then there are those who try to discredit the green movement and justify exploiting the environment for profit.

Finally, the green movement is being forced to accept a form paradigm regression, in the form of sustainable development.

WHAT DOES THIS MEAN FOR THE EVALUATION OF LITERACY LEARNING?

In our explorations we discovered that similar things were happening in literacy and in the evaluation of learning. Table 1.1 shows how we think similar kinds of things are happening to literacy education.

Table 1.1: Old and new paradigms of literacy education

Old paradigm	New paradigm
Emphasis on simplifying the complex act of literacy by fragmentation into subskills which are mastered according to a predetermined sequence	Emphasis on helping learners understand how all the subsystems of language work together to create meaning
Literacy is made up of a unique and independent set of language skills (reading, writing, talking, listening) which stand alone as subjects in their own right	Reading is one of the many parallel forms of language and has a strong symbiotic relationship with writing, speaking, listening and other forms of language
Belief that one single 'correct' meaning is fixed within texts	Belief that meaning is socially constructed, and that constructing meaning from text is a process of transaction between text and reader
The primary purposes for teaching literacy are communication of meaning and acquisition of information from printed texts	The primary purpose for teaching literacy goes beyond communication. It also includes helping learners gain control of language for purposes of critique, access to power, social equity, and social change
Literacy is best acquired in tightly defined sequential 'stages' or 'levels' which can be identified, measured and quantified for all learners	Literacy is best acquired holistically. Fragmenting and separating the skills and knowledge that make up literacy artificially distorts the whole learning process and seriously complicates the acquisition of literacy.

Table 1.2 shows how the same logic can be applied to evaluation.

Table 1.2: Old and new paradigms of assessment and evaluation

Measurement-based 'old' paradigm	New or 'emerging' paradigm
Emphasis on ranking learning through use of quantitative numerical measures such as scores, grades, levels, etc.	Emphasis on understanding learning through use of qualitative concepts and 'measures'
Insistence that 'objectivity' is both possible and necessary	Recognition that 'objectivity' is not achievable. Emphasis on acknowledging and then controlling subjectivity
Use of standardised instruments to measure 'amounts' of learning that have been acquired	Emphasis on and faith in the 'human-as-instrument'
Emphasis on reporting using numbers and/or numerically based devices such as grades, levels, bands, etc.	Emphasis on reporting in qualitative terms, usually in narrative text.

So what? How does this help us understand why assessment and evaluation have become such controversial issues in education circles?

We believe that what lies at the core of much of this (often heated) debate is related to the concept of *paradigm shift*. It seems that the prevailing paradigm of evaluation has not kept pace with the emerging paradigm of language and learning. When you have a conflict situation like this, there can be no productive result. Instead, whenever there is a lack of congruence there is frustration, uneasiness, and lack of clarity. It is like having a nut and a bolt with different threads and expecting them to fit together comfortably and support each other in the task of holding things together. We know that when this happens force is often used (we use a hammer to force them to fit). As a consequence the whole (the nut and bolt together) becomes dysfunctional.

We came to realise that the prevailing paradigm of evaluation of student learning is in the 'old/traditional' mould, while the prevailing paradigm of language education is in the 'new/emerging' mould. While there has been the equivalent of a paradigm shift in approaches to language education, the evaluation of student learning is in a state of paradigm paralysis. Betts (1992) defines paradigm paralysis as the 'attempt to interpret current experiences using old models and metaphors that are no longer appropriate or useful' (p. 38). He equates it with a condition labelled 'mumpsimus', which Webster defines as 'persistence in a mistaken belief'. We believe that this condition aptly describes the current state of what we call 'evaluation of student learning'. Table 1.3 summarises this state of incongruity.

Table 1:3: Incongruity between paradigms

Paradigm of language and learning language	What this meant for teaching practice	Paradigm of evaluation
Language learned from whole to part; holistic, naturalistic view of learning. Language is functional.	Classroom strategies and activities reflect beliefs about learning and language learning.	Traditional testing: standardised tests; teacher-made tests — learner is either right or wrong. Errors not tolerated. Product focus.

Table 1.3 suggests that the paradigm shift in the field of language education has been a three-pronged one. **Firstly** there has been a shift away from what could be labelled a 'fragmented' view of language education to a more 'holistic' view in which language is highly functional and cannot be fragmented into bits, as each part is contingent on the whole. This shift has brought with it a shift in emphasis from a focus on the end products of acts of language to a more predominant focus on the processes that lead up to those end products. **Secondly** there has been some intense questioning and re-examination of the traditionally held 'habit-formation', behavioristic views of learning. This questioning and re-examination has resulted in a shift toward what could be called a more 'naturalistic' view of learning. **Thirdly** there has been a strong shift in the model of language on which curriculum designers have based the curriculum. Instead of an eclectic mix of prescriptive traditional Latin-based grammar, infused with some overtones of Chomsky's transformational grammar, there is now a strong emphasis on Halliday's functional model of language. When these three prongs come together, the result is a view of language education that varies from what has been traditionally held.

This 'coming together' is what we understood holistic learning/teaching to be. However, the prevailing paradigm of evaluation is more suited to the old/traditional view of language education as a series of separate subskills that have to be learned in preplanned, linear sequences of individual skills.

This lack of congruence which seemed to exist between what we believed about learning, language, and language education and the prevailing paradigm of evaluation and assessment in our school system and the community created great tensions. What was needed (we believed) was a situation in which there was a high degree of congruence between our language-education beliefs and practices and our assessment and evaluation beliefs and practices. Table 1.4 summarises what we considered to be a more congruent state of affairs.

Table 1.4: Congruence between paradigms

Paradigm of learning and learning language	What this meant for teaching	Paradigm of evaluation
Language learned from whole to part; holistic, naturalistic view of learning Functional view of language	Classroom strategies and activities reflect beliefs about learning and language learning	An approach to evaluation which draws information from the context of the classroom; assessing what each student can do or is attempting to do; process is valued

The challenge for us was how the congruence demonstrated in Table 1.4 could be achieved. What paradigm of evaluation best 'fitted' the paradigm of language education within which we were working? How could we get an assessment and evaluation 'nut' that had the same thread as the language/ literacy education 'bolt' we were trying to fit it on? What could we do to prevent paradigm regression and resist the pressure that comes from those who cannot make a paradigm shift — those who seem prepared to argue strongly for a return to traditional ways of thinking about language education that 'fit' with the prevailing (traditional) paradigm of evaluation?

This is the focus of the next chapter.

2

Getting a nut and bolt with the same thread

Matching evaluation theory with language learning theory

by Jan Turbill

The preface describes how a 'developing sense of uneasiness with traditional methods of evaluation that we were expected to employ' brought us together. This developing sense of uneasiness was expressed in the comments teachers made when asked why they were willing to participate in the project. Their responses clearly indicated that it was a problem of 'fit' between evaluation theory and language education theory. When teachers tried to apply the methods and procedures inherent in the 'old/traditional' paradigm of evaluation to the 'new/emerging' paradigm of language education they experienced many difficulties. They made such comments as:

'... it seems wrong to separate evaluation from teaching and learning. I can't understand why my principal forces me to take half of every Friday to stop teaching and give all these weekly tests.'

'I'm unhappy about basing my evaluation on the reading test we use or on a one-draft piece of writing done under pressure. Neither tell me very much about the processes involved.'

'I have this intuition that the kids themselves ought to be part of the evaluation, shouldn't they?'

'I know more about each of these kids' abilities to read and write than the formal tests we use can ever hope to reveal, but that's being subjective isn't it? I learned in my pre-service training that subjectivity is wrong ...'

'These tests have no relationship to the goals and expectations that I have in language.'

'In my class I have the opportunity to really find what my kids know and think as they are actually engaged in the process of learning. I'm sure that would be more effective than any of the tests I'm currently using, wouldn't it?'

9

When we collaboratively reflected on comments such as these we agreed that we were implicitly seeking an approach to the evaluation of language learning which would:

- bring learning, teaching and assessment back together;
- focus on process as well as product;
- include the learner, and other traditionally ignored stakeholders as part of the process;
- acknowledge the enormous superiority of the 'knowledgeable-human-as-instrument' over the 'formal-test-as-instrument';
- be as rigorous, credible and trustworthy as the traditional measurement-based paradigm of evaluation;
- make use of data which were collected while the students were engaged in the learning contexts that teachers created rather than in specially created 'testing' contexts.

The question we had to resolve was:

Is there a theoretically sound paradigm of evaluation that could fulfil these criteria?

We looked around in the everyday world, hopeful that we could identify an approach or model of evaluation that would effectively meet these requirements.

We were attracted to the way that parents seem to evaluate their children's growth and development in the world outside classrooms. Parents, for example, are constantly interacting with their children and intervening and participating in the various activities that they undertake each day. They get the opportunity to observe their offspring engaged in a wide range of behaviors. They are continually gathering data about their children's growth and development from these activities. When called upon to make judgements about the child's developing maturity (to be 'accountable') they can usually pull together all that they've observed and make an accurate report.

What makes this possible? As we reflected on this question we made many connections. For example, we realised that parents spend sustained periods of time both observing and interacting with their children. Furthermore, they have a special relationship with their children. The role is a mixture of caregiver, nurturer, teacher, helper, director, decision-maker, evaluator. Fundamentally they are **responsible for** and **responsive to** the needs, wants, concerns, issues that are part of being a child and growing up in a culture. Typically they help their children acquire that culture by **participating** in their learning, not by teaching them using a teacher-dominated, direct instructional pedagogy. This 'teacher-as-participant' role is not dissimilar to what we call 'co-researching'.

It is through this process that children are acculturated, (learn/acquire their culture). Because children have typically bonded with their parents and other caregivers an authentic, caring relationship develops. It is through this role of 'participant' that parents and caregivers evaluate their children's development using their understanding of cultural expectations, cultural norms, and child development to assist them. In a sense they are not unlike participant observers who use what they observe to make value judgements about what they see and hear. Whereas researchers who take a participant observer's role usually are seeking to understand some esoteric research-based problem, parents' focus is 'how is my child developing according to the expectations and standards of my culture?'

Parents are also unconsciously aware that the relationship they have with their children may bias or prejudice how they interpret what they see and hear. They have everyday ways of trying to control this subjectivity. This is why they tend to sample their children's behavior across different contexts, bouncing their interpretations of what they see off others, such as spouses, neighbors, grandparents, other parents with similar aged children. If they have a serious concern or burning issue that relates to their offspring's development they seek another more expert opinion, such as the clinic nurse, the doctor, or the child development section of popular magazines. This kind of activity helps them triangulate their information. It forces them to rethink their interpretations, and often modify them.

Furthermore, parents have an implicit but coherent theory of how maturity and/or growth should proceed in children in their culture and they know what to look for. They obviously have a set of 'pointers', 'indicators', 'signs' or 'markers', of maturity that guide their observations against a set of standards or benchmarks of maturity at certain ages.[1]

What are these markers? Where do they come from? There are the obvious 'broad' indicators such as learning to walk, learning to talk, getting a first or second tooth, losing a tooth, and so on. Then there are more specific ones such as being able to use a telephone, riding a bike, rejection of the Santa Claus myth, and hundreds of others which illuminate and inform each child's development. These indicators are a function of the parents' knowledge and

---

[1]We have decided to use the term 'markers' which we regard as synonymous with 'pointers', 'indicators', 'signs'. We define 'markers' as 'behaviors which mark that the child has achieved a certain outcome. These outcomes can be organised into broad levels which can be called 'benchmarks' or 'standards'

understanding of child development. Those who have most knowledge and understanding of this domain have access to many more indicators than those whose knowledge is less complete. As they become more experienced, their theories of child development change, along with the indicators they use. This is another way of saying that experts not only know more than novices, they see more too.

What are the key components of this everyday day model of evaluation? In summary they include at least the following:

- a purpose for evaluation (in this case to respond to stakeholders' concerns about their offsprings' growth and development and be responsible for ensuring that it continues in appropriate ways);
- opportunities to gather information from uncontrived, naturally occurring settings;
- opportunities to observe, interact, intervene, and participate in whatever is being evaluated (in this case something called 'development');
- a special relationship with those they are evaluating;
- a commitment to respond to the needs and concerns of their children;
- a strong feeling of responsibility for setting up contexts which will facilitate their children's development;
- a theory of what appropriate or good development is;
- a set of markers that they can recognise in their child's growth and development;
- a set of strategies and/or resources for dealing with their subjectivity and bias.

We began to look around for a model of evaluation that had these features.

RESPONSIVE EVALUATION

We discovered that there is an analogue to this parental model in the research literature. It was pioneered by Stake (1975), extended and modified by Guba and Lincoln (1981, 1985, 1989), and called **responsive evaluation**.

Responsive evaluation is a model of evaluation that has formally and systematically organised all the characteristics listed above. It is theoretically similar to the investigative methods that ethnographers, anthropologists, sociologists and investigative journalists use to understand, evaluate, and develop practical theories which can be used to explain whatever phenomenon they are focused on. It is strongly based on a naturalistic, qualitative approach to research.

In responsive evaluation the evaluator is expected to become involved in the situation and gather information from those who are being evaluated, in order to respond to their needs and concerns. This is usually done by talking to them, observing them in action and collecting various 'artifacts' (products, outcomes) from the various situations that are observed. The more we studied the formal set of principles which characterised the formal theoretical system known as responsive evaluation, the more similarities we found with the kind of evaluation that is continually being carried out in the everyday world. Just as in everyday evaluation, responsive evaluators must have:

• a purpose for evaluation (to respond to stakeholders' concerns about whatever is being evaluated, and be responsible for ensuring that the responses result in appropriate outcomes for all stakeholders);
• opportunities to gather data from uncontrived, naturally occurring settings;
• opportunities to observe, interact, intervene, and participate in whatever is being evaluated (in this case something called 'language learning');
• a special relationship with those they are evaluating;
• a commitment to respond to the needs and concerns of their students;
• a strong feeling of responsibility for setting up contexts that will facilitate their students' literacy development;
• a theory of what appropriate or good language/literacy development is;
• a set of markers that they can recognise in their students' literacy growth and development;
• a set of strategies and/or resources for dealing with their subjectivity and bias.

When the fundamental characteristics of each form of evaluation are compared there is a very high degree of similarity between the two as Table 2.1 shows.

Typically, responsive evaluation has been restricted to the evaluation of large curriculum initiatives and/or educational programs. It has not been used to evaluate school-type learning in individual students. We believed that the principles which underpinned responsive evaluation could be applied to the evaluation of individual student learning in literacy classrooms. Furthermore, as we came to understand it better we became convinced that these principles 'fitted' our paradigm of language education comfortably. We believed that we had found a robust and strong thread which could pull together our evaluation 'nut' with our language education 'bolt'.

As we studied the methods and processes used by responsive evaluators we were convinced that teachers could:

(i) create similar opportunities
(ii) use similar kinds of procedures to evaluate their students' language development

This is not to say that many teachers had not already begun to move in this direction. For example many of our co-researcher teachers had been engaged

Table 2.1: Responsive evaluation in and out of school

Fundamentals of responsive evaluation in the everyday world	Fundamentals of responsive evaluation in literacy
• a purpose for evaluation	• a purpose for evaluation (in this case to respond to stakeholders' concerns about individual students' literacy development and be responsible for the ensuring that such responses result in appropriate outcomes for all stakeholders)
• opportunities to gather data from uncontrived, naturally occurring settings	• opportunities to gather data from uncontrived, naturally occurring classroom settings
• opportunities to observe, interact, intervene, and participate in whatever is being evaluated	• opportunities to observe, interact, intervene, and participate in whatever is being evaluated (in this case something called 'language learning')
• a special relationship with those whom they are evaluating	• a special relationship with those whom they are evaluating
• a commitment to respond to the needs and concerns of those being evaluated	• a commitment to respond to the needs and concerns of their students
• a strong feeling of responsibility for setting up contexts that will facilitate the required outcomes	• a strong feeling of responsibility for setting up contexts that will facilitate their students' literacy development
• a theory of what appropriate or good outcomes are	• a theory of what appropriate or good language/literacy development is
• a set of markers that they can recognise	• a set of markers that they can recognise in their students' literacy growth and development
• a set of strategies and/or resources for dealing with their subjectivity and bias	• a set of strategies and/or resources for dealing with their subjectivity and bias

in something called **portfolio assessment** since the writing revolution in the 1980s. More recently, many had begun to implement a method of reporting to parents known as **negotiated evaluation** (Woodward 1992).

Portfolio assessment grew out of the need to collect samples of students' work, particularly writing samples. Teachers used this information to prepare reports for parents. Negotiated evaluation grew out of the need to find better ways of reporting to parents. This focus led teachers to consider what information they needed to collect and how they could best store it. It seemed that these two approaches had originated from opposite ends of an evaluation continuum. However, as teachers explored and refined these approaches they began to move towards each other until it was difficult to distinguish one approach from the other.

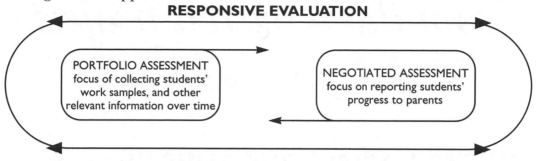

Figure 2.1: Where portfolio and negotiated evaluation 'fit' with responsive evaluation

We believed that what was missing in both approaches was a theoretical framework. Neither portfolio evaluation nor negotiated evaluation provided teachers with a framework of evaluation, or a framework of language education which helped them interpret and make sense of the information they collected in consistent or coherent ways.

We believed that responsive evaluation provided such a framework because it was congruent with the paradigm of learning we wanted to apply in our classrooms. If we were to evaluate the learning that results from the application of this paradigm, we needed a paradigm of evaluation which supported it.

We believed that we had found it.

3
What we found out from the research project

by Brian Cambourne & Jan Turbill

THE NEED FOR SOME CRITERIA OF EFFECTIVE EVALUATION

It became obvious when we began the process of sharing meanings that many of us had different notions of what constituted 'effective' or 'good' evaluation. We realised, as we tried to make explicit what we thought effective evaluation looked like in practice, that this was something we had taken for granted (everyone knows what effective evaluation is), but had never really thought too deeply about.

We recognised that unless we could at least tentatively agree on some working definitions of effective assessment and evaluation we would not get very far. Therefore, as well as developing shared meanings about what the terms 'assessment' and 'evaluation' meant, we decided to try to come to agreement on the nature of effective assessment and evaluation.

We soon discovered that it was not easy to determine what constituted effective assessment and evaluation. After much reading, discussion and debate, we agreed to these criteria as a tentative basis for beginning the project.

Criteria of effective assessment and evaluation

- Assessment and evaluation must result in optimal learning for all involved.
- Assessment and evaluation must inform, support and justify teacher decision-making.
- Assessment and evaluation practices must reflect the theories of language, learning and literacy which guide our teaching.
- The findings that result from our assessment and evaluation practices must be accurate, valid, reliable, and perceived to be rigorous by all who use them.

Assessment and evaluation must result in optimal learning for all involved.

In one sense this is a motherhood criterion. Everyone would agree that it is a 'good' thing to have an assessment and evaluation procedure that results in optimal learning for all. It is almost impossible *not* to agree with such a laudable criterion. It's what lies behind it, the things that it presupposes that we found difficult. We had to address such issues as 'What is optimal learning?', 'Who should be included in the "all"?', 'Who should benefit from any evaluation that is carried out?'

It didn't take us long to realise that we couldn't address the question 'What is optimal learning?' until we had sorted out what effective reading, writing, language development, learning, etc., were. This forced us to examine our values and beliefs about learning, literacy, language, and teaching. We discovered that not all of us had the same ideas about what 'optimal learning' actually was. Neither did we agree on who should comprise the 'all'. The fact that we didn't share the same beliefs about these things did not prove to be a hindrance. We realised that we could tolerate differences of opinion in these areas, as long as we had gone through the process of trying to make them explicit for ourselves and each other. Chapters 3, 4 and 5 describe examples of different teachers' attempts to address this question.

Assessment and evaluation must inform, support and justify teacher decision-making.

The previous criterion 'Optimal learning for all' influenced the generation of this one. We strongly believed that among those who should optimally learn from any evaluation procedure should at least be the teacher who is doing the evaluation, the learner being taught, and the learner's parents. We could see little point in an evaluation procedure that doesn't help teachers, learners and parents make good decisions about what should be done next. For example, a diagnostic test of reading given to children late in Grade 6 when they are about to transfer to secondary school, where most of the teachers are subject specialists who are unlikely to make use of this kind of information, is not good evaluation practice.

Assessment and evaluation practices must reflect the theories of language, learning and literacy which guide our teaching.

We agreed that there was little benefit from teaching in a way which, for example, encouraged learners to go through the process of drafting, revising, editing and proofreading to produce a piece of writing, and then evaluating what has been learned by making the learner compose a one-draft, perfect piece without the opportunity to draft, revise and edit. We could see no point in encouraging young learners to use the 'have-a-go' strategy in spelling and then evaluating them on a right/wrong basis. In fact, any evaluation practice that was not congruent with the way we taught language could only serve to send mixed messages to learners, which could only confuse them. How could optimal learning for all result from such incongruity?

The findings which result from our assessment and evaluation practices must be accurate, valid, reliable, and perceived to be rigorous by all who use them.

The teachers who participated in this study were all aware that the prevailing paradigm of evaluation was one which insisted that evaluation could only be valid if it was measurement-based, objective and had something called 'high reliability'. Many of them had done courses such as Statistics 101 while at university, and were uncomfortable about using assessment and evaluation procedures which could be labelled 'subjective', 'biased', 'unreliable', 'soft' or 'invalid'. They also realised that many of those to whom they were accountable (parents, principals, system-wide administrators, policy makers, resource-givers, politicians, etc.) were locked within the measurement-based paradigm and could be highly critical of any approach to evaluation that had even a tinge of subjectivity or 'softness' about it. Therefore we decided that this criterion was fundamental to any assessment and evaluation procedure. Unless we could demonstrate that the procedures being used were at least as 'scientific' as measurement-based evaluation, then they would not result in optimal learning for all.

HOW TO BECOME A RESPONSIVE EVALUATOR

In the five years the project ran we generated a great deal of information. In what follows some of this information is summarised.

The map of the journey

A 'big picture' of what is involved in the journey from fumbling novice to skilled responsive evaluator at the classroom level emerged. We identified what appear to be 'stages', 'phases' or 'interim destinations' in this journey. We also discovered some basic processes that served as 'bridges' between stages. In keeping with the 'journey' metaphor we developed a conceptual map of this journey, shown in Figure 3.1. The different stages are in boxes and the bridging processes that lead from one stage to the next are set between the boxes.

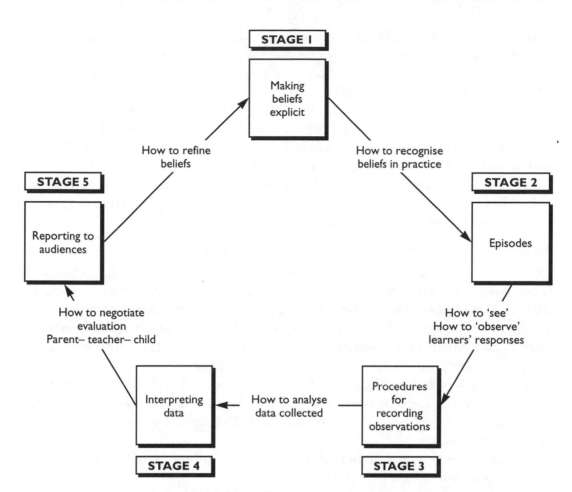

Figure 3.1: The conceptual map of the journey

Figure 3.1 is a summary of the understandings, knowledge, and skills that the co-researching teams discovered they needed if they were to implement responsive evaluation effectively. We have come to the conclusion that any staff development program which does not include at least these fundamentals will not be adequate for teachers to learn responsive evaluation.

This map is the result of drawing together the multiplicity of experiences that occurred as we made our way towards understanding what we were trying to do. We also need to emphasise that the processes we went through didn't occur sequentially. We didn't begin with 'Stage 1' on the map — 'Making our beliefs explicit' — before dealing with what we've called 'Episodes' and then moving on to 'How to see, How to observe learners' responses', and so on.

When we ran into difficulties we would slow down, back up, and ask, 'What's missing?' 'What else do we need to do'? Each time we did this we came to the same conclusions: some knowledge, understandings, skills, were prerequisites of others. For example, we all eventually had to ask ourselves some fundamental questions about what we really believed about literacy. Having done this, we then had to work out how to recognise these beliefs in the daily ebb and flow of classroom teaching. This in turn meant that we had to work out how to look at our teaching. Did we look at 'lessons'. Did we look at 'periods'? Did we look at 'sessions'? How could we organise ourselves to assess and evaluate without stopping teaching?

All this led us to the concept of episodes. This in turn forced us to think about how to collect information, but before this we had to learn how to 'see', how to observe learners' responses; and so on around the map.

Stage 1: Making our beliefs explicit

One of our big discoveries was the crucial role that tacit knowledge (intuition, unverbalisable know-how, unconscious understandings, values, beliefs, ideology, etc.) played in the processes of assessment, evaluation and teaching. We began to discover the way that implicit beliefs and values about learning, literacy, language and evaluation influenced how we taught, why we taught what we taught, and how, why and what we evaluated.

As we proceeded in the project we experimented with some techniques which seemed to help us begin the journey. Essentially, they were techniques that forced us to reflect on what we believed. The simplest of these was to ask these questions:

1. What is effective literate behavior? (spelling, reading, writing, etc). Why?
2. How is it best acquired? Why?
3. After it is acquired, what should it be used for? Why?

At first these questions produced motherhood-type answers such as 'Good reading is reading for meaning'. We found it necessary to help the teachers going thought this process to make several more cuts at the question ('Why do I believe that good reading is reading for meaning?'), and when they had answered that to ask again 'Why do I believe that?', gradually peeling away the layers until they reached what one of them called an 'an inner core which I couldn't cut into any more. Then I knew what I really believed and why I believed it.'

Bridging procedure 1: How to recognise beliefs in practice

Once we had started to bring our values and beliefs to conscious awareness and share them with each other, we realised that these would become the bases of how we would eventually judge whether or not our learners were achieving what we really believed they should be achieving in the name of literacy. If, for example, we decided that 'good reading was being able to comprehend texts from a range of different genres' we had to find out what this looked like when it occurred. *We had to learn how to recognise our beliefs in practice.*

This forced us back to our classrooms. We spent a long time revisiting the videos and field notes we took of each other trying to recognise, from the complexity of things that happen in classrooms, concrete evidence of 'good reading' as we defined it. We found that in order to do this we had to move on to a second stage of the journey.

Stage 2: Episodes

We found that we had to develop a different way of describing the way teachers organised their time. The traditional concept of 'the lesson' that lasted for a prescribed unit of time (say 15 minutes in lower grades and 30–45 minutes in higher grades) and that had a prescribed sequence of 'steps' was not an accurate way of describing how these teachers organised time. We found that language sessions were much longer (up to two hours) and were organised by much larger units than the lesson. We decided to call these units episodes. Our co-researchers gave these episodes names such as 'teacher reading', 'SSR', 'workshop' and 'sharing'. Table 3.1 shows an example of this kind of organisation.

Table 3.1: An example of episode analysis

Episode organisation – Grade 5 fully integrated 2-hour daily language session		
Timing	**Episode**	**What happens**
15-20 minutes	Whole class focus	Teacher reads, models, demonstrates reading, writing, spelling, etc. Children engage with demonstration in a range of ways.
15-20 minutes	Print walk	Teacher takes students on guided tour of wall print in room and demonstrates structure and function. Children engage, respond.
20-30 minutes	Sustained silent reading (SSR)	Children select books and read silently.

Timing	Episode	What happens
50 minutes	Activity time	Children work on contracts and activities individually and in groups. Teacher conferences with as many as possible.
10-15 minutes	Demonstration time	Teacher demonstrates skills, understandings to whole class/small groups.
10-15 minutes	Sharing time	Children share insights, drafts, books, problems, issues with rest of class. Class members respond and comment. Teacher listens, occasionally intervenes with comment or refocus.

This process was very effective for helping teachers deal with the logistics of organising time and resources for collecting information. We found that while every teacher in the project was able to complete this task, no two did it in exactly the same way. For example, we found that the way teachers sequenced their episodes was idiosyncratic. Some teachers divided their sessions into more episodes, others less. No two teachers sequenced their episodes in exactly the same way. While some used the same names, other labelled their episodes in unique ways.

Bridging procedure 2: How to 'see'; How to observe learners' responses

At this point we found the concept of 'episodes' useful for helping us organise ourselves for Stage 3. We realised that before we could begin to collect information or record observations, we had to know what we were looking for. We had to learn how to 'see' and observe learners' responses.

In order to do this, we combined the processes we had used to make our beliefs explicit, (the three questions listed above) with the notion of 'episodes', and worked our way through the sequence of activities listed in the box opposite:

1. Focus on one episode.
2. Ask and answer the question: 'Why do I have this episode in my daily schedule?'
3. Ask and answer the question: 'What data-gathering procedures (i.e. assessment procedures) can I employ during this episode that won't break into or stop the flow of teaching and learning?'
4. Ask and answer the question: 'What markers can I use during this episode that will inform me that students are/are not learning within this episode?'
5. Ask and answer the question: 'What sense or meaning can I make from what I collect?'

This process was very effective for helping teachers achieve three things:
- it further helped them make explicit their beliefs, values, and ideologies about literacy;
- it helped them begin to understand the stages or interim destinations on the conceptual map;
- it began to help them deal with the logistics of organising time and resources for controlling all the various 'pieces' that make up effective responsive evaluation.

Table 3.2 is an example of what the process looked like.

Table 3.2: Unpacking an episode

Episode	Why I have episode	Possible markers I can look for	How I can assess in episode
SSR	• Sustained engagement with written text provides students with valuable practice in reading. • Opportunities are provided for reading a wide range of genres. • Reading own choice of book at own pace develops positive attitudes to reading.	• Time taken to select book. • Depth of engagement in book (facial expressions, eye movements, page turning, oblivion to noise, reluctance to leave book). • Number of books completed. • Number of pages completed in any one episode. • Student's personal rating of book in log.	• Observations recorded as comments in field notebook. • Observations recorded per checklist. • Students' reading logs.

In this example the teacher has chosen to focus on an episode she calls sustained silent reading (SSR) and has listed some of the reasons she has for making SSR a regular classroom episode. For example, she believes that it is important that learners be given the opportunity to engage with written text in a sustained way for sustained periods of time as it provides valuable time for practising reading, and has therefore written *Sustained engagement with written text provides students with valuable practice in reading*.

She also believes that students should get control of a wide range of written genres, and she uses SSR time as a means of providing opportunities for her learners to choose from a range of different genres. Therefore she's written *Opportunities for reading a wide range of genres are important*.

She also believes that a positive attitude towards reading is crucial if her learners are going to become life-long readers: *Reading own choice of book at own pace develops positive attitudes to reading*.

In the next column, she has begun to identify some of the markers of effective literate behaviour that she would be looking for during the SSR episode. She has decided that one good marker is the time students take to choose a book when SSR time begins, because she believes that the time taken to select a book is one marker of how well students have learned to read the blurb, browse through the opening pages and make decisions about what to read. These latter behaviors are also markers in their own right.

She has also listed *deep engagement with text* as another behavior that can be a marker of effective reading behavior. If we examine this broad marker in more depth we see that there are a whole range of markers that show deep engagement — facial expression, how the eyes move across the page, the way the pages are turned, being oblivious to extraneous noises or disturbances, reluctance to put the book down, whether the reader changes books frequently, and so on. It is also possible that some of the markers of deep engagement could be used as markers of 'enjoyment' or a 'positive attitude'.

She has also written *number of books completed* and *number of pages read* as markers. This is because she believes that speed of reading, especially if accompanied by evidence of comprehension of the author's intended message, is another important marker of growing reading ability.

Note, too, that she's included *How students rate books which they've read* as a marker. She intends to ask the students to rate the books they complete on a five-point scale and then ask them to justify this rating when she conferences with them during Activity Time.

In the final column, she's begun to identify some possible assessing procedures that can be done as part of the episode and which she could use to collect and record evidence of the presence or absence of these markers.

Observation is an obvious assessing procedure that can be used during an episode like SSR, so she has listed *Observations recorded as comments in field notebook*. Because she has also developed her own checklist for observing reading behaviors, she has also listed *Observations recorded per checklist*.

Because she believes believe that students should be expected to take some responsibility for collecting information, she has designed a simple page on which students could record such things as what they read, how much they liked it, how many pages they read, how long it took them to complete a book. She calls this page a reading log. Therefore she's also listed *Students' reading logs*.

It is important to note that these markers, and ways of collecting evidence for them, all reflect this teacher's values and beliefs (ideology) about what an effective reader should be able to do. For example, she believes that good readers should be able to engage with texts for sustained periods of time. Another part of her ideology is the belief that good readers move along fairly steadily and has therefore included 'number of pages read' during SSR as a marker. The decision to include a rating scale as part of the student's responsibility also reflects part of her ideology, that is, the belief that comprehension is a desirable outcome of reading, and that being able to justify why one likes or doesn't like a book is a good marker of deep comprehension.

Bridging procedure 3: How to analyse data

Teachers who become responsive evaluators are just like researchers, in the sense that they must interpret the information they have collected. If we are not to be choked by the information we collect, we must be able to organise it in a way that reduces its complexity and makes it manageable; otherwise it becomes useless. This process is more fully developed in Chapter 8.

Stage 4: Interpreting data

Before we could begin to interpret data we had to learn some skills and techniques of data analysis. We found that simply gathering information (Stage 3) was only one part of the assessment and evaluation process. Unless we could use the information to inform ourselves and others about the learning which had (or had not) taken place, then simply gathering information (no matter how rich) was not much use.

Bridging procedure 4: How to negotiate evaluation — parent–teacher–child

Once we had identified who the major stakeholders were we realised that if we were to be truly 'responsive' to their concerns we had to work how to include them in the process. Likewise, it was obvious that if the reports we were going to make available to the various audiences to whom we were accountable were going to result in 'optimal learning for all', we had to be able to negotiate with them about what it was they were concerned about. This was one of the most crucial bridging procedures we had to develop. Chapters 6, 9 and 10 deal with this bridging procedure in more detail.

Stage 5: Reporting to audiences

After interpreting the information that has been collected, we need to report it to the different people who have a stake in the child's learning. While there are many possible stakeholders, three that all agreed should all be included were the parent, the teacher and the child.

One of our group used a triangle metaphor in her assessment and evaluation plan.

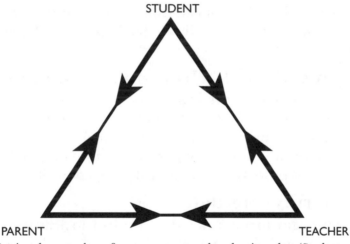

Figure 3.2: A triangle metaphor of an assessment and evaluation plan. 'Students, parents and teachers should operate as a team in order to enhance the learners' realisation of educational and lifelong goals. Lines of communication need to be opened and strengthened with opportunities for sharing knowledge made available.'

Bridging procedure 5: How to refine beliefs

We found that this process was cyclic, and that it didn't stop after one trip around the map. The processes involved in this kind of assessment and evaluation force teachers to constantly reflect and refine their beliefs, impacting on the rest of the processes and destinations on the map; after a few journeys around they find their beliefs becoming tighter and clearer.

SO WHAT DOES THIS MEAN FOR ASSESSMENT AND EVALUATION AT THE CLASSROOM LEVEL?

We believe that we are beginning to identify a staff development process which will enable teachers to implement, describe and justify a rigorous, scientifically 'respectable' approach to assessment and evaluation that is congruent with the principles underpinning the theories and practices of language teaching that we currently value. These initial findings have been used to develop a finely tuned staff development program which has been trialled in NSW and the USA. This program captures the essential features of what we have worked through as co-researchers.

Our data are beginning to show that going through the processes identified in this research forces teachers to begin the exploration of values and beliefs about learning and teaching, and the beginning of the identification of markers of effective learning. This, in turn, provides insights into how classrooms might be organised and managed within the outcomes framework which was mandatory for these teachers. It also starts the journey toward confidence and empowerment that begins to emerge when teachers work their way through the processes encapsulated in this model.

In the following chapters many examples of this model in action are provided by teachers who worked through these processes.

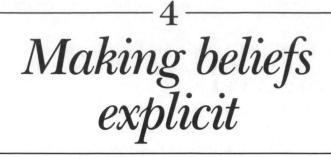

4

Making beliefs explicit

One teacher's journey

by Vonne Mathie

This chapter provides an example of what one teacher's belief system looks like when it is changed from a vague kind of unverbalisable know-how into a set of definitive principles that can be can be articulated clearly and cohesively by the one who owns them. Our research shows very clearly that when teachers are given the opportunity to share, discuss, and reflect as part of a supportive community of co-learners, they become much more confident, self-assured, and in control of what they do in the name of assessment and evaluation.

While working in this project I was moved by the words of a popular song written by the late Harry Chapin. This song highlighted the potential impact that teachers' beliefs and values about the world of learning can have on a students' attitudes, skills and knowledge development. The song was motivated by a school report that Chapin's son brought home from school. Included in the report was this comment:

Your son marches to the tune of a different drummer. But don't worry we'll soon have him joining the parade by the end of the year.

This report caused Chapin to do what thousands of parents have done over the years — question the purposes of the school experience for the learner. Unlike many other parents he could comment on this in a unique way by writing a popular song about it. The song describes two teachers with different sets of beliefs about how children should paint a picture. One demands that the child 'paint things as they are'; the other allows some creative interpretation. The first teacher's advice became the chorus for the song:

Flowers are red, Green leaves are green
There's no way to see them any other way
Than the way they always have been seen

[Popular song from the 70s by Harry Chapin]

One teacher (the one whose point of view became the chorus for the song) represents those teachers who place themselves at the centre of the classroom curriculum or program. Their focus is on teaching the selected knowledge and skills to their students (controlling the transmission). Their students are expected to accept, digest and, at specific times, recall or perform in ways considered appropriate by either the teacher or the system. Within such a setting the student could be described as a passive recipient.

The other teacher represents those teachers who place the student at the centre of the classroom curriculum or program. Learners and learning are their primary foci — they perceive their major role as that of facilitator, not only providing opportunities within the learning process for student discovery and problem-solving, but also providing the appropriate support and encouragement, which is the essential ingredients for fostering a stimulating and non-threatening learning environment. Within this setting the student could be described as an active participant.

Beneath the words of this song I found this message:

Teacher behaviors are a reflection of teacher beliefs. Teacher beliefs drive teaching and learning practices (including assessment and evaluation techniques and procedures).

My purpose in this chapter is to:
- describe the processes that helped me to bring my values and beliefs to conscious awareness
- present these beliefs and elaborate on them

MAKING MY BELIEFS EXPLICIT

The process I went through to make my beliefs explicit was time consuming, at times difficult and frustrating and, on a few occasions, painful, but ultimately highly worthwhile. Essentially it meant trying to identify and then verbalise the intuitions I had been developing over years of classroom experiences, study, and the action research I had conducted at different times in my career.

In order to begin in this process I needed:
- a set of questions that focused my thinking and caused me to dig deeper and deeper into my pool of knowledge, values, and experiences
- a community of fellow learners (co-learners)

A set of questions to focus thinking

The questions I found most helpful in focusing my thinking went through a couple of stages. In the very early stages of the project I asked myself questions that forced me to look closely at what I actually did each day in my class, for example:

- What kind of classroom environment am I creating and maintaining? Why?
- What learning outcomes am I aiming towards or encouraging within that environment? Why?

I spent about one term (10 weeks), one afternoon per week, videoing myself in action, looking at these videos, usually with my co-researching colleagues, discussing what we saw in the light of these two questions, reflecting on them, revisiting the videos, more discussion and reflection, and so on. With this kind of help I was able to get a good picture of what I was doing and the kinds of explicit and implicit messages I was giving to my students.

Having clarified and documented the 'what actually happens' dimension in my classroom, I had to explore the 'what should happen' dimension. In order to do this I had to change focus; first I had to go right back to basics. Like the rest of the group I had to work at three basic questions:

- What is literacy?
- What does it mean to be literate?
- What is the most appropriate model or theory of learning that will help me produce the kind of literate students I want to produce?

A community of co-learners

In a community of co-learners, each co-learner must be prepared to be involved in 'personal and collaborative reflection, discussion, planning, sharing and refining of ideas and practices for collecting and analysing information about student learning.'

EXPLICIT BELIEFS

What I found out about myself and the notion of literacy

I spent some time dealing with the questions 'What is literacy?' and 'What does it mean to be literate?'

At the beginning of 1992, I posed those questions to a number of people of different age, gender and occupation. Overall, the responses represented a narrow, rather shallow view of literacy, for example:

A person is literate when they are able to read and write.

A person is literate when he or she can read and write and understand well enough to survive and/or cope in our society.

It is not so long ago that my own view of literacy was equally as narrow and shallow: 'literacy is the written component of language'. However, my recent experiences have caused me to view literacy from a broader and deeper perspective and I now feel very comfortable with the definition of literacy expressed in the IYL Paper No.2:

Literacy involves the integration of listening, speaking, reading, writing, and critical thinking; it incorporates numeracy. It includes cultural knowledge which enables a speaker, writer or reader to recognise and use language appropriate to different social situations ... our goal must be on active literacy which allows people to use language to enhance their capacity to think, create and question, which helps them participate more effectively in society.

Previously I had considered literacy to be a subset of language, incorporating only the written component. Now I would argue quite differently. For example I now believe that:

- language (listening, speaking, reading and writing) is used by people in a variety of ways to meet their specific needs and specific purposes, at specific times in specific contexts. All of these ways of using language is literacy;
- literacy is a society's life blood. Literacy enables a society to function effectively, to grow, to heal, to meet new challenges, to solve problems and to overcome difficulties. It is essential for learning and communicating with the personal, commercial, economic and political structures of that society.

These understandings helped me see that literacy is specific to the different cultures within a society. A specific literacy evolves within each culture in response to specific needs. People learn the literacy of their culture by simply being members of it and so the literacy that people develop may render them literate in one culture, yet illiterate in another.

This in turn helped me realise that there was a crucial relationship between content (knowledge), culture and literacy. Previously I had viewed the content of my class curriculum merely as a vehicle through which literacy could be developed, but I had failed to recognise three factors that play an important role in determining the effectiveness of that development:

- the way in which my culture and ideology influenced my actual selection of content for my class program;
- the way in which my culture and ideology influenced the way I presented that which I had selected;
- the 'what' of my evaluation and why it was important for me to evaluate.

Once I understood the connection between these factors I then understood how teacher selection and presentation, because it typically represented the dominant mainstream culture, could seriously disadvantage learners from minority groups. Furthermore, I came to believe that for a classroom environment to foster effective learning for all learners, much depended on whether teachers had developed an awareness of the learners' cultural backgrounds that in turn influenced their planning, implementation and evaluation.

These insights led to other insights, and the following are some of the most important.

- That the gradual development of critical literacy means the gradual empowerment of more members of the society, which in turn means that more members of that society are in a position to bring about change that will make for a fairer, more equitable society. I became aware of the possibility that literacy could become a tool that could be used to gain access to power, which could be threatening to those who want to keep power to themselves.
- That if teachers have only a shallow understanding of literacy and its purposes, then the learning experiences they provide for learners will have a narrow, superficial, and non-critical focus. If, on the other hand, they develop deep understandings about literacy and its purposes they will create environments that produce the highly critical, literate students we all value.
- That my expectations of my students, the way I set up my classroom, the way I assess and evaluate my students' learning should reflect *my* beliefs about literacy, learners and learning.
- That my beliefs, therefore, should be made explicit, for they ultimately determine the quality of the teaching and learning environment I will create and maintain, and my interpretation of the mandated outcomes.

Making my beliefs explicit like this was a slow continuous process. It was, however, a very professionally rewarding and empowering one, and only made possible through the 'co-learning' process. One other belief I've developed through this process is that all staff development should be based on this model.

What I found out about myself and the notion of learning

As I analysed the data I'd collected from my classroom each week, I realised that I held a very 'messy' model of learning. It seemed to be a mixture of many different bits and pieces from books and inservice courses I'd attended during my professional life. I began to look around for a theory of learning that was more consistent and which 'fitted' my emerging beliefs about literacy. I found myself attracted to a theory of 'everyday' or 'natural' learning — sometimes called 'whole learning', 'integrated learning', or 'comprehensible input'. (Cambourne 1988, Cambourne & Turbill 1990)

This theory of learning asserts that durable, powerful, and complex learning continually occurs outside of school because of the conditions available to learners in natural settings. It argues that if we could simulate these conditions inside the classroom we could achieve similar kinds of successes. So what are these conditions? What do they mean for me?

Although Cambourne (1988) provides a systematic explanation of this theory, I found that I had to expand and on some occasions modify many of these conditions to make them my own. I called the result 'my language plan'.

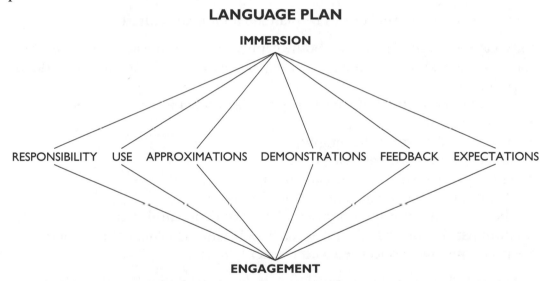

Figure 4.1: My language plan

Immersion: Learners need to be immersed in whatever it is they want or need to know. For language, this could include oral and written genres. It can also include all other semiotic systems, such as visual art and drama.

Demonstrations refer to the multitude of examples, both written and oral which a learner needs in order to develop control of whatever is the focus for their learning at any particular time.
Demonstrations:
• should be planned but can also be spontaneous
• should be meaningful

- can be provided by a variety of people
- need to be repeated and recycled

I learned that there was a very strong relationship between quality teaching and the quality of the demonstrations that are provided. I am convinced that meaningful, comprehensible demonstrations lead to quality learning. Unfortunately, the obverse is also true. Meaningless, incomprehensible demonstrations lead to confused or inadequate learning.

Feedback refers to the responses that learners get from significant others in the learning environment, both teachers and fellow-learners. Feedback:
- is a response to a need
- should be positive
- must be constructive
- should confirm and/or promote learning
- is individual
- can occur 'on the run' or can be planned and/or structured

Expectations are messages, both explicit and implicit, which teachers communicate about learning, learning behaviors, and individual students. Expectations:
- are conveyed by the ways teachers act, talk and behave
- should be positive
- must be realistic and challenging
- can be different for each child
- set the ground rules for the classroom
- establish the learning climate in the classroom

The three conditions — demonstration, feedback and expectations — are predominantly concerned with teacher behavior. The next three conditions are predominantly concerned with learner behavior.

Responsibility refers to the need to help learners realise that they should be able to make some learning decisions for themselves. Responsibility means that learners must accept some responsibility if they are to become independent learners.

My own experiences have convinced me that learning best occurs when learners can make some decisions about what, when and how they will learn. I believe that some teachers remove responsibility from students by telling, rather than judiciously questioning.

Use (practice) refers to the need for learners to be given time and opportunity to use and practise their developing control of whatever it is they are learning. Use/practice:

34

- should be regular
- should be realistic, functional and comprehensible
- should be positive and honest

Approximations refer to the learner's attempts to gain control of some process, knowledge, skill or understanding. I used to believe that approximations were 'errors' which had to be identified and rooted out before they became permanent fixtures in the learner's repertoire. Now I believe that they are a natural part of learning and are very informative both to me and the learner. Approximations:

- should be viewed as markers or indicators of development
- often indicate a need which requires a demonstration
- should be encouraged
- must be understood by learners as an important part of the learning process

Immersion refers to the quantitative dimension of this kind of learning. The higher the degree of the immersion in whatever it is that is being learned, the more chance there is that the learning will be effective. In language classrooms it refers to the degree to which the environment is saturated in written and oral language that is used constantly to help learners solve the language puzzles they are faced with each day.

Engagement refers to that moment in the learning process when the learner attends to the salient features of a demonstration for the express purposes of internalising and learning what is being demonstrated. It cannot be consciously engineered. Deep engagement with demonstrations is more likely to occur when all the other conditions are in place.

What I found out when I pulled all this together

With the help of my co-learners I gradually pulled together a 'big picture' of what would make a classroom an effective learning setting, given the beliefs that I had made explicit. I called this 'my personal model of the effective literacy learning classroom'.

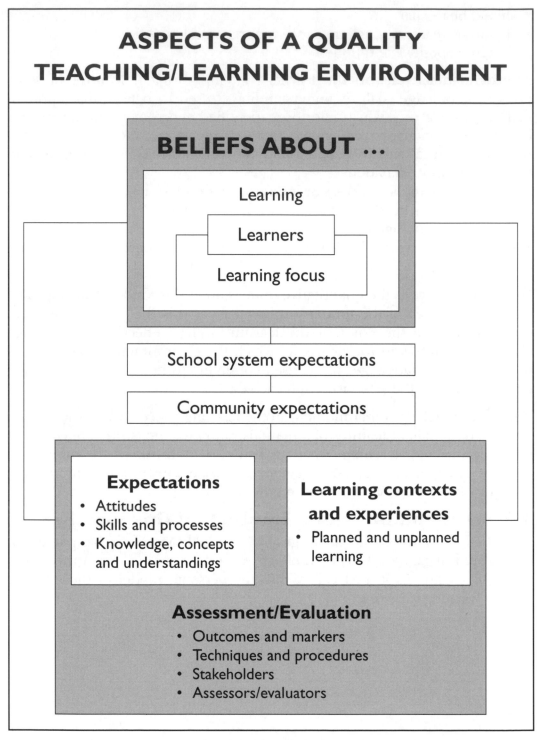

ASPECTS OF A QUALITY TEACHING/LEARNING ENVIRONMENT

BELIEFS ABOUT ...

Learning

Learners

Learning focus

School system expectations

Community expectations

Expectations
- Attitudes
- Skills and processes
- Knowledge, concepts and understandings

Learning contexts and experiences
- Planned and unplanned learning

Assessment/Evaluation
- Outcomes and markers
- Techniques and procedures
- Stakeholders
- Assessors/evaluators

Figure 4.2: My personal model of the effective literacy learning classroom

Expectations: These include the teacher's expectations of students' acquisition of attitudes, skills, processes, knowledge, concepts and understandings.

Learning contexts and experiences: This is where both planned and unplanned learning occurs.

Assessment & evaluation: This includes the outcomes, markers, techniques, procedures, and the stakeholders.

Beliefs: These include teacher beliefs about learning, learners and the learning focus (in this case literacy).

I believe that the 'beliefs' component plays the most significant role of all. It is the crucial factor which ultimately determines the expectations, learning contexts and experiences, and assessment and evaluation programs. Teacher beliefs are reflected in teacher practices which determine the teaching/ learning environments. These, in turn, determine the quality of the teaching/ learning environment.

CONCLUSION

I now consider myself to be an effective evaluator of my students' learning. The processes I use to collect and interpret information and then report it to the various people who have a right to know fulfil all the criteria of effective evaluation listed in Chapter 3. I can justify in persuasive language that what I do is scientifically respectable and valid. However, this state of affairs and the sense of empowerment that comes with it would not have been possible without taking a big breath and asking myself the hard questions — those which forced me to explore and confront the beliefs and values that drive my teaching. The sense of empowerment that I now have comes from knowing why I do what I do in the name of assessment and evaluation.

The first step in this journey had to be making my beliefs explicit. I strongly believe that all teachers who want to be similarly empowered must take this first step.

5
Organising the classroom for responsive evaluation

Getting started K-3

by Janelle Graham

In Chapter 4, Vonne Mathie described how she went about making her beliefs explicit. Our research shows that this is the first stage in the journey to becoming an effective responsive evaluator. Mathie concluded that for her this is the most important stage of the journey.

But what comes next? According to our conceptual map of the journey, there are a number of concepts that need to be turned into classroom action, including 'How to recognise beliefs in practice', 'Episodes', 'How to see and observe learners' responses' and 'Procedures for recording observations'. All these destinations could be grouped under the heading 'Organising the Classroom'.

In this chapter Janelle Graham, a K-3 teacher, describes how she organised her classroom as she wrestled with the nitty-gritty details of organising herself using the principles that lie behind each of these concepts. Janelle writes from the perspective of one who has just begun the journey.

BACKGROUND

I had been teaching for 15 years when I first became interested in responsive evaluation. I had been a classroom teacher in four different primary schools, teaching all grades from Kindergarten to Year 3.

Since 1987 I have been teaching at Nowra East Primary School, a large school with enrolment exceeding 600 students. The school receives federal government funding support from the Disadvantaged Schools Program

(DSP) due to the low socio-economic nature of the community it services. In addition, about 20% of the students at this school identify themselves as Aboriginal, entitling further federal funding through the Aboriginal Student Support Parent Awareness (ASSPA) Program and the Priority Schools Program (PSP).

GETTING STARTED: THE BEGINNINGS OF INTELLECTUAL UNREST

As a classroom teacher endeavoring to implement a class program based on the principles underpinning what some refer to as 'natural learning' (Cambourne, 1988), and what others refer to as 'whole learning' (Cordeiro 1992), 'everyday learning' (Resnick 1987) or 'comprehensible input' (Krashen & Terrell 1983), I came to an uneasy realisation that, although I was able to support my students with meaningful learning experiences, my assessment and evaluation procedures did not always sit comfortably with what I believed about learners. There was a gap in my understanding. I became concerned about the learners in the classroom environment I had created, and I realised that this concern emerged from a vague sense of uneasiness with traditional measurement-based methods of evaluation. I found it incongruous to impose a test at the end of a learning unit and use it as the sole instrument of evaluation. I felt that such tests were an imposed situation which did not give good information, especially about the children who did not belong to the predominant mainstream culture. I was especially concerned about the Aboriginal children in my class.

At the beginning of 1991 I was teaching 30 students in a composite Kindergarten/Year 1 class when I became involved in an exciting and innovative co-researching program which presented a vehicle for me to develop congruence and cohesion between what I believed and my teaching practice. This project focused on evaluation procedures and techniques and seemed to me an excellent and worthwhile opportunity. I joined a team of four teachers from my school who became my co-researchers in the project.

WHAT I DID: MY EXPERIENCES IN THE PROGRAM

Like Vonne Mathie (Chapter 4) I had to look at what I was doing in my classroom and establish how my students were growing in language. Like her I needed the supportive climate provided by co-researching and, like her, I met each week with my co-researchers and discussed the videos, field notes and the reflections I made in my journal.

Co-researching:

I can see a need to investigate assessment of children which really reflects the way children are taught. There is such an incongruity between teaching whole language and then assessing children by standardised tests. So I see a need.

Co-researching provides an incredible support structure for investigations in the classroom. Jan guides me through my own learning experience.

It can be overwhelming to think of the whole task that lies ahead. Seeing other people who have struggled and coped is good — obviously time is huge part of the process.

The biggest problem for me has been jumping onto the moving platform. Hesitation at the unknown!

Figure 5.1: Reflections from my journal

Regular debriefing sessions helped me to articulate and explain my classroom practice and stretched me to my limit as I delved into reflective practice. My co-researchers encouraged me to organise, clarify and refine my beliefs, instructional practice and evaluation techniques and procedures. It was a continuing cyclical process which Figure 5.2 succinctly captures.

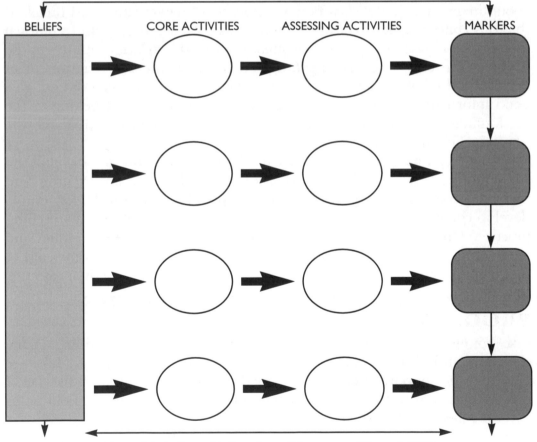

Figure 5.2: J. Hancock's flow chart of the process (Hancock 1991)

Through this continuing cyclical process I adopted, adapted, developed, refined and reorganised to suit the ever-changing needs of my students and myself. Figure 5.3 shows the beliefs that resulted from this process.

Explicit beliefs

•   Young children have the ability to grow more each day. There are recognisable markers in their development. Yet each child is an individual. Intervention and interaction at the point of need is important.

•   Children become more empowered as they move through this process and learn how to gain control of language.

•   Young learners need encouragement. 'Failure' is a big setback. 'Encouragement is what makes champions' (John Newcombe).

•   Young learners need a supportive environment. They will respond when needs are recognised and met, and guidance is provided.

•   The teacher is not the only authoritative source in the classroom. There are 31 teachers in my classroom and 31 learners.

•   Children learn a lot from their peers — by listening, observing and interacting. This is a powerful example for them.

•   Parents are valuable resources.

•   Set standards for work presentation, ground rules and routines are essential. Children need to be able to organise and take responsibility for themselves. Let everyone see consistency, firmness, yet fairness.

•   Quality not quantity.

•   Literacy is a tool for learning.

Figure 5.3: My beliefs

WHAT NEXT? THE NITTY-GRITTY DETAILS OF ORGANISATION

The remainder of this chapter focuses on my language session and how I assess for language learning. One of the first things I had to do was to identify the episodes I typically used to structure my language session. Because of my beliefs about the necessity to keep learning whole and comprehensible I was careful not to fragment this session into artificial segments like traditional 'lessons'. I wanted the session to operate as a set of related and integrated learning experiences for my children in which I could teach all the skills and knowledge associated with literacy in ways that helped them make the connections between the big picture and the small bits. I found that I typically organised my language session into four episodes:

• teacher reading
• drop everything and read (DEAR)
• reading focus
• writing focus

Figure 5.4 shows how these were organised and what kinds of activities/ materials I typically used in each episode.

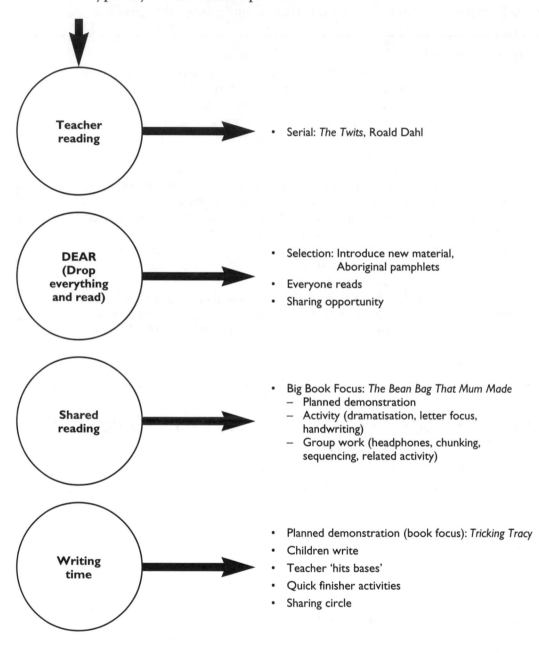

Figure 5.4: Teaching episodes

Assessment procedures: the techniques I used to collect information

I use a variety of procedures to collect information, each chosen to fit in with the teaching activity I was engaged in. For example, during teacher reading I was engaged in reading a book and demonstrating the skills and strategies of reading. My time in this episode was fully taken up with this task and it would have been very difficult to do this effectively and mark off a checklist of behaviors that I was interested in. All I could do was observe informally some of the behaviors of the children as I read to them and try to retrospectively record them in note form at the end of the episode. I could also ask some children to retell what they'd heard from time to time.

However, in an episode like DEAR I was not so involved in demonstrating, and so had more time to collect information. Consequently I had the time to take field notes, set up a video, interact with children, and so on. This organisation is set out in the Figure 5.5.

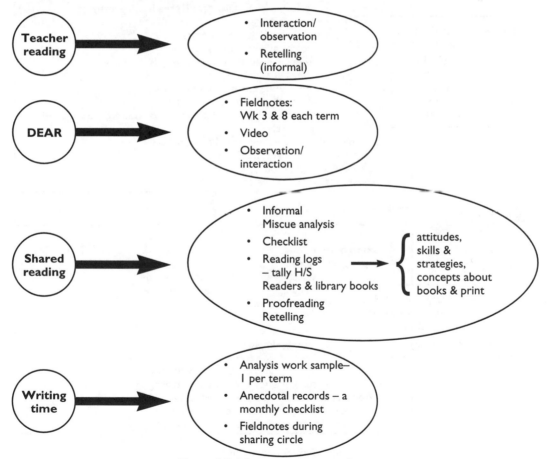

Figure 5.5: My assessment procedures

How to recognise beliefs in practice

After deciding on assessment procedures that were appropriate for the role I played in each episode, I had to decide what to look for. I needed to be able to recognise 'cues' that would provide evidence that the children were engaging with what I demonstrated in each episode, and were actually learning and developing as a consequence. Some of my co-researchers called them 'markers', others called them 'indicators', some called them 'criteria of achievement'. I decided to call them 'engagement cues'. (The official K-6 English syllabus refers to them as 'pointers'.)

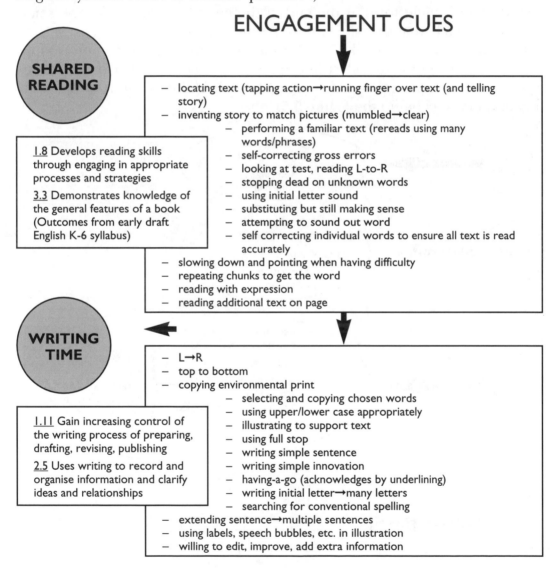

ENGAGEMENT CUES

SHARED READING

1.8 Develops reading skills through engaging in appropriate processes and strategies

3.3 Demonstrates knowledge of the general features of a book (Outcomes from early draft English K-6 syllabus)

- locating text (tapping action→running finger over text (and telling story)
- inventing story to match pictures (mumbled→clear)
    - performing a familiar text (rereads using many words/phrases)
    - self-correcting gross errors
    - looking at test, reading L-to-R
    - stopping dead on unknown words
    - using initial letter sound
    - substituting but still making sense
    - attempting to sound out word
    - self correcting individual words to ensure all text is read accurately
- slowing down and pointing when having difficulty
- repeating chunks to get the word
- reading with expression
- reading additional text on page

WRITING TIME

1.11 Gain increasing control of the writing process of preparing, drafting, revising, publishing

2.5 Uses writing to record and organise information and clarify ideas and relationships

- L→R
- top to bottom
- copying environmental print
    - selecting and copying chosen words
    - using upper/lower case appropriately
    - illustrating to support text
    - using full stop
    - writing simple sentence
    - writing simple innovation
    - having-a-go (acknowledges by underlining)
    - writing initial letter→many letters
    - searching for conventional spelling
- extending sentence→multiple sentences
- using labels, speech bubbles, etc. in illustration
- willing to edit, improve, add extra information

Figure 5.6: Engagement cues

The flow chart in Figure 5.6 captures the processes I went through. Fundamentally, I tried to combine my own beliefs about effective literacy learning with the profile statements in the draft English K-6 syllabus we were working from at the time, and then asked myself this question:

Given these beliefs and these profile statements, what behaviors might occur in this episode that will provide evidence of successful and/or unsuccessful learning?

I have given an example of some of the profile statements (these are numbered as in an early draft the English K-6 syllabus and shown in the smaller boxes to the left) and some of the 'engagement cues' I could look for to confirm (or deny) that successful learning was occurring.

PUTTING IT ALL TOGETHER

In what follows I will attempt to fill in the 'big picture' of what all this looks like in action by describing what typically happens in each one of these episodes and relating it to the assessment procedures I used.

Teacher reading

I like to begin each language session by reading to the students. Not only am I able to provide a vital role model, but it is also an important time to expose students to good quality literature and to examine the many facets of author craft. Teacher reading provides students with an opportunity to develop pictures or images in their minds using the spoken word. In the older grades I read a serialised text. In Kindergarten and Year 1 I may use a poem, picture book or nonfiction text, depending on the current unit of classwork. I have gradually developed a set of assessment procedures for this episode. These include:

• observation and interaction
• rating scale

Observation and interaction

This is ongoing. While I am engaged in the process of reading I try to interact with students, noting observable nonverbal cues such as facial expression or laughter; oral responses to questions; participation during discussion and informal retelling of significant facts or happenings.

Rating scale

This is used periodically. Our rating scale has evolved from a simple 'smiley' or 'sad' face to a five-category scale which has an accompanying list of descriptive words to help students make a personal response to a text.

great   O.K.   ordinary   not so good   horrible

excellent terrific   boring

Figure 5.7 Rating scale

As my confidence increased I encouraged children to write further elaborative reviews which uncovered their feelings and opinions. I like to humanise the authors and illustrators and demonstrate that the processes involved in their writing is exactly the same for us in our classroom too. Recently I encouraged my class to send their review of a text to the author in an effort to make the activity more meaningful.

Dear Diana, I like yor book I reckon it is great I have my on oon Fat and Juicy Place myn is in a trala I sum time I play in it in the rfd noom rfda school.

from chris

N EPS
Jervis
Street
Nowra
2541
2 4 93

Figure 5.8: Samples of reviews. These were sent to the author.

I believe students need to be included in the process of their learning and that providing opportunities for them to explore their attitudes in a supportive environment should be paramount. Learning is more than the acquisition of content and facts. Recently I asked my students to tell me why it is important for the teacher to read to them. I wanted to see what they thought. Some answers were:

- so everyone can learn to read
- by listening I can find the same books and read them
- so I can learn to read and write
- I can learn to read properly
- I get better at reading
- the teacher knows how to pronounce the words we don't
- reading gives me good ideas
- when you read we know more
- so we can learn

Drop everything and read (DEAR)

I like to follow teacher reading with a DEAR time. I believe students learn to read by reading, therefore I provide an opportunity during a busy day for quiet individual reading. I make sure there is plenty of good quality reading material that the children can read including nonfiction, fiction, picture books, poetry books, song books and class-made books. I establish a routine, demonstrate selection strategies and introduce new material; however, students are encouraged to exercise personal choice.

I have become aware of the importance of providing a role model and so I always read when the students are reading, even if there are pressing needs such as money to collect, books to check, desk drawers to tidy.

When I first started to take DEAR time seriously and understand its importance and potential I realised that I needed and wanted to be able to have evidence of student's growth and development. In contrast to the teacher reading episode, DEAR provided the opportunity for me to 'step back' and begin to closely watch what my students were doing.

Early in the project my awareness of the cues of development was brought about by making many sets of field notes and video-taping episodes with my co-researchers. I was able to look at the data and see repeated the many little behaviors which indicated engagement in reading behavior. Initially I didn't see and couldn't identify many cues. It was only when I noticed the same actions being repeated by different children that they became more apparent and I realised that before this I had been using them subconsciously. In order to formalise these behaviors I recorded them as cues on a list, although it was impossible to put them into a precise order of attainment as each child moved in his/her own way along a continuum of development. Episodes like DEAR lend themselves to a relatively simple method for collecting data for evaluation, namely the taking of field notes, and these can be used as rich source of evidence of children's learning.

As I became more familiar with the cues of development I began to formalise an assessment procedure that allowed me to document each student's progress. Now during weeks 3 and 8 of each term I take field notes during DEAR time. I tell the students that I am not going to read on these days. Instead I will be writing about what they do.

As I grew in confidence I decided to provide opportunities to involve the children in their own learning. I began to read my field notes aloud and asked students to add any details I may have left out. I found that my students were honest and willing to add details. Now during weeks 3-8 I am able to document cues which tell me about their growth as indicated by the achievement of the particular learning outcomes I was required to use. These field notes also help to confirm or reject the evaluative conclusions that I begin to draw from data that I have collected from other episodes.

I have found an unexpected spin-off from this process. My understanding and knowledge of the early school years is helping uncover more cues and I'm aware that I am gradually constructing a continuum of developmental cues that are my own, that are congruent with my beliefs and the mandated profiles, and that are easy to use, and help me articulate and justify what conclusions I draw about each student's learning. For example, I have always believed that knowledge of parts of a book and purposeful selective reading are important benchmarks of development. Because of the processes involved in becoming a responsive evaluator I have observed some children using the contents section of nonfiction books to turn to the section they are interested in. This becomes a valid and reliable cue for these two skills. Ultimately, I use observations like this to develop my own checklist so that I can see overall development and growth.

Name: _Kathy Gardiner_   Class: _2·10_

			June	Nov
EMERGENT		Able to listen to stories	✓	✓
		Can match one to one	✓	✓
		Able to identify high frequency words	✓	✓
		Can recognise difference between capital letters and lower case	✓	✓
EARLY		Willing to 'have-a-go'	✓	✓
		Uses meaning as a cue	✗	✓
		Uses structure as a cue	✗	✗
		Uses pictorial cues	✓	✓
		Able to recognise similarities in words	✓	✓
		Recognises he/she has made an error	✗	Sometimes
		Able to self-correct	✗	Sometimes
		Can make predictions	✓	✓
		Can retell a story (orally).	✓	✓
FLUENT		Is able to read silently		
		Reads with expression		
		Selects suitable reading materials		
		Differentiates between fiction and non-fiction		
		Shares with others		
		Makes generalisations about characters and story		

	June	Nov
Borrows frequently from Home / School readers	✓	✓
Borrows regularly from school Library	✗	✗

Figure 5.9: An example of a checklist

Reading focus

This episode centres around the shared-book strategy. It provides opportunities to focus on the demonstration of skills and strategies for reading, as well as the development of understandings of concepts about books and print. I believe that peers provide one another with powerful examples and I use the strengths of individuals to build on to the learning of their classmates. A continual assessment program gives me an insight and understanding of individual strengths and weaknesses, resulting in a more meaningful and directed learning opportunity. I incorporate a variety of strategies for gathering data for assessment and evaluation including:

• informal miscue analysis (1 per term)
• checklists (1 per term
• informal retelling (ongoing)
• reading tallies (1 per term)

Informal miscue analysis

As I listen to and watch each child read a text I record their behavior and any markers which indicate they are engaging in the process of reading. I don't just tape-record students reading, as interaction and observation are vital. A young reader's expressions and eye movement give evidence of the skills and strategies they are using to decode print. (Figure 5.10)

Checklists

These are completed in conjunction with an informal miscue analysis and used to record incidental information gained through observation and interaction. (Figure 5.11)

Informal retelling

During and after a shared-book experience I check with students by getting them to retell the story in their own words. This gives me further data on which to base my evaluation.

Reading tallies

To indicate student and sometimes parental interest in reading, I incorporate a record of book borrowing through both the optional (though actively encouraged) school library borrowing program and my class's home/school borrowing program.

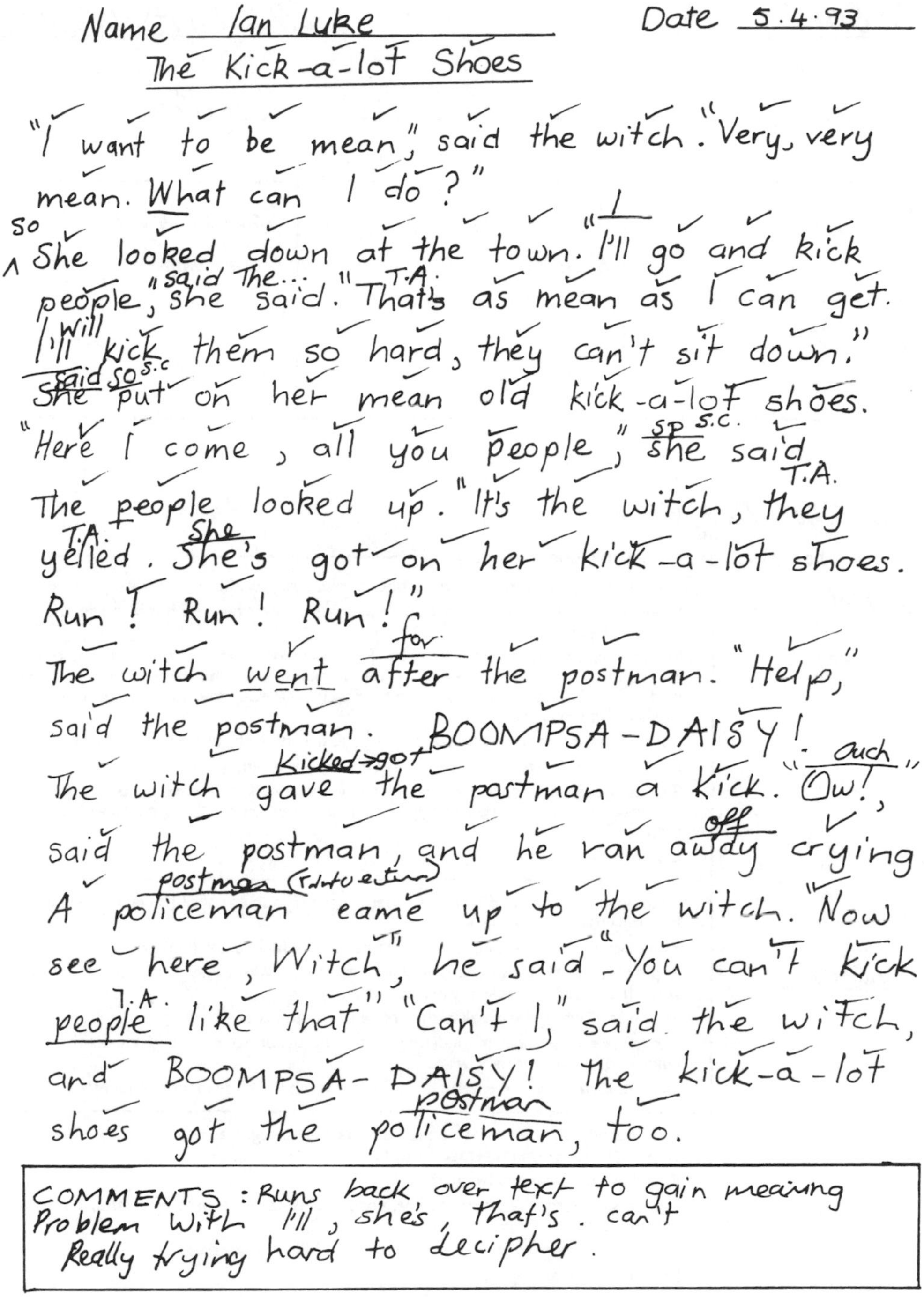

Name __Ian Luke__   Date __5.4.93__
    The Kick-a-lot Shoes

"I want to be mean," said the witch. "Very, very mean. What can I do?"
So
∧ She looked down at the town. "I'll go and kick people," she said. "That's as mean as I can get.
I'll kick them so hard, they can't sit down." She put on her mean old kick-a-lot shoes.
"Here I come, all you people," she said.
The people looked up. "It's the witch, they yelled. She's got on her kick-a-lot shoes.
Run! Run! Run!"
The witch went after the postman. "Help," said the postman. BOOMPSA-DAISY!
The witch gave the postman a kick. "Ow!," said the postman, and he ran away crying.
A policeman came up to the witch. "Now see here, Witch," he said "You can't kick people like that" "Can't I," said the witch, and BOOMPSA-DAISY! the kick-a-lot shoes got the policeman, too.

COMMENTS : Runs back over text to gain meaning
Problem with I'll, she's, that's. can't
Really trying hard to decipher.

Figure 5.10: Informal miscue analysis

YEAR ONE   ENGLISH ASSESSMENT

Name _____ Class_____

Attitude:	Home/School Reading:	School Library Borrowing:
Knows letter names:		

Informal Miscue Analysis —

The following behaviours arise from this understanding:

Emergent Readers	Enjoy listening to stories, handling books, discussing books and stories.
	Frequently ask to hear stories aloud and request their favorite books be read over and over again.
	Perform fluently from favorite books. They focus on retrieving the meanings of the book. In order to do this they rely on their memory for the story and the language of the text. They are often able also to match what they say with the appropriate pages in familiar books.
	Locate front of book and follow page sequence throughout on familiar books.
	Locate print on pages and distinguish between print and pictures.
	Self correct gross errors occasionally e.g. when they know when parts of a story have been omitted or are wrongly sequenced or when the language doesn't sound right.
	Experiment with writing.
Early Readers	Read word by word and often use their finger to point as well (careful checking of positional/directional cues).
	Pause when reading if they come to something which is unfamiliar or difficult.
	Repeat words, phrases or longer segments of text when they come to a difficulty or when they need to confirm their accuracy.
	Self correct when they realise they have made an error.
	Recognise some words immediately – their attention to visual detail leads them to build a vocabulary of sight words.
	Show enjoyment and excitement in their own ability to read independently.
Fluent Readers	Read fluently on appropriate texts because they integrate cues almost instantly to construct the precise message from print.
	Recognise many words by sight.
	Shift to slow word by word reading, finger pointing and pauses when they confront difficulties.
	Read increasing quantities of new and more difficult materials.
	Self correct when appropriate.

Figure 5.11: Checklist developed through miscue analysis

Writing focus

Every episode leading up to writing focus has provided demonstrations. I program this episode last because I like to immerse the students in a multitude of demonstrations before they put pen to paper. This episode begins with a whole-class demonstration when children are actively encouraged to help contribute as the writing is constructed. This planned demonstration incorporates the skills and strategies of the writing process, including spelling, grammar and handwriting, and responds to those observed needs of students made apparent through the assessment and evaluation procedures. These procedures are incorporated into the episode and not just tacked on. The assessment procedures I typically find easy to apply in this episode include:

- collection and review (monthly)
- sampling analysis
- writing analysis sheet (1 per term)
- proofreading sample (1 per term)
- sharing circle field notes (ongoing)

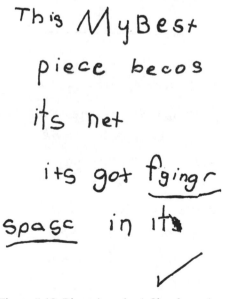

Figure 5.12: Bianca's review of her best piece

Collection and review

While students are writing, I interact and conference with them, often using this opportunity to record engagement information on the back of their piece of work. At the end of each month all samples of work are collected.

During a class discussion or on an individual basis, students choose the piece that they like the best. The students are expected to explain why they think that piece has merit. Other children may comment and give encouragement at that time. (Figure 5.12)

Sampling analysis

Older grades record their choice on a proforma sheet which includes space for comments about spelling strategies. (Figure 5.13)

Name _____

Date _____

My favourite piece of writing is

_____

Date _____.

Because _____

_____

_____.

When I write I ...

O find words in the classroom.
O use classroom books.
O use the dictionary.
O ask a friend.
O have-a-go.
O use personal word box.
O ask Miss Graham.
O other

Figure 5.13: Proforma sheet for older grades (1-2)

Writing analysis sheets

I select one piece which I think most clearly indicates the greatest development. Figure 5.14 is an example.

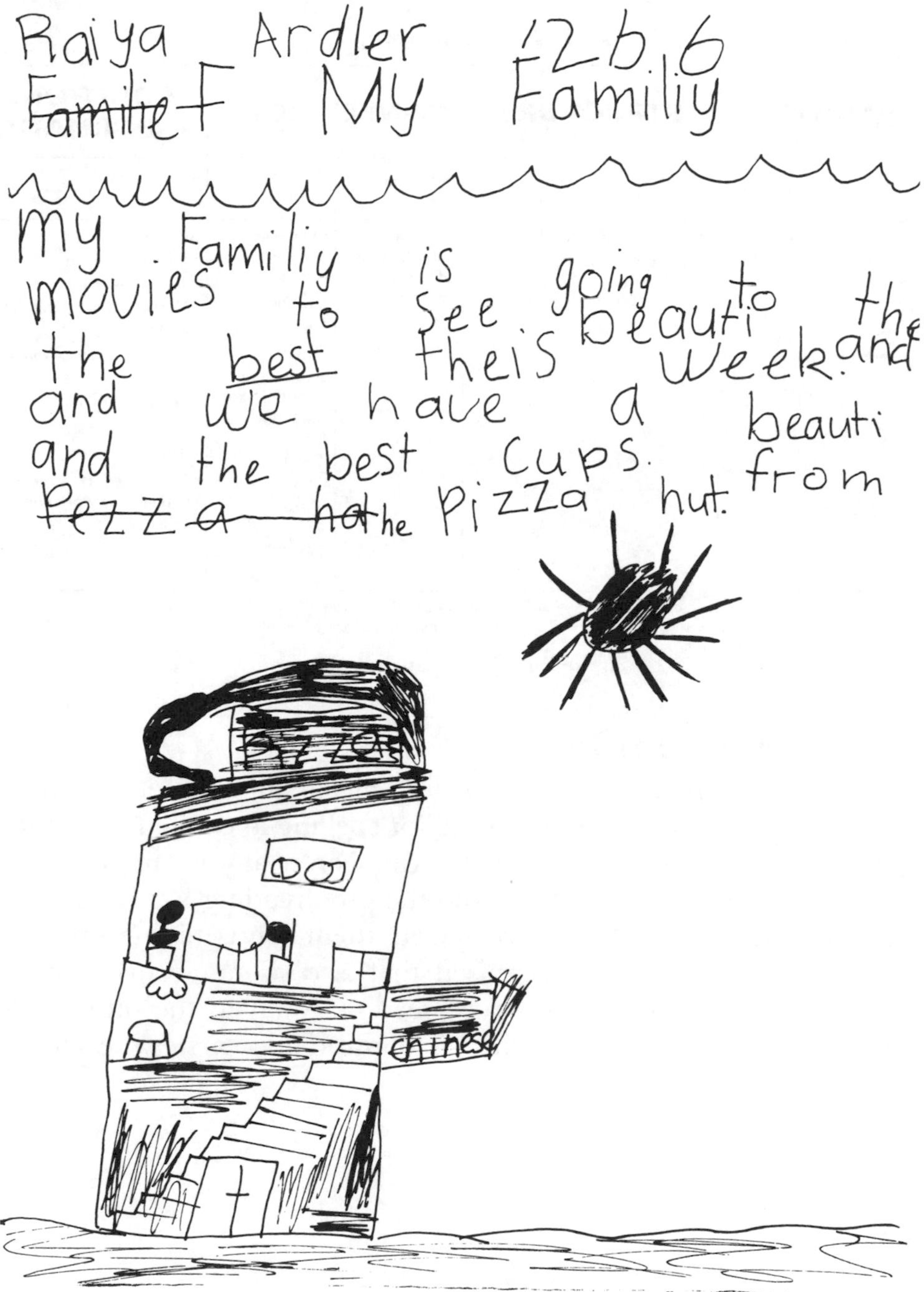

Raiya Ardler 12.6.6
~~Familief~~ My Familiy

My Familiy is going
movies to see theis beauti to the
the <u>best</u> theis week.and
and we have a beauti
and the best cups. from
~~Pezz a hot~~he Pizza hut.

Figure 5.14: Raiya's best piece for the term

55

I complete a writing analysis sheet which includes room to comment on a wide variety of strategies used during writing. There is a space to include the student's individual observed need/s.

NAME: RAIYA ARDLER   TEXT: Free choice   DATE: 26/6

MEANING	STRUCTURE	CONVENTIONS		ADDITIONAL INFORMATION
		Punctuation/ Grammar	Spelling	
A recount of a planned trip to the pictures and a visit to the Pizza Hut Clear-extended piece used • environmental print • letter sounds • memory	• Titled piece 'My Family' • Kept adding information to text. Overrode full stops.	Used full-stops but later added additional information.	• Underlining have-a-go words • adding 'ing' • 'beauti' (beauty) Scrounged this from the book she brought in for news – 'Beautiful Biscuits'. • Letter sounds 'best'→beast 'theis'→this	June: • Follows on from demonstration • Work becoming colorful and much neater • Recognising unconventional spelling • Humor • Labels illustrate • Titles • Sometimes stay at desk continuing to work during sharing circles

Observed Need: • Punctuation – use of full stops   Adding extra information
                  • Extra time for writing??   Eliminate over use of an

Figure 5.15: Raiya's analysis sheet

Proofreading samples

A representative sample is selected to indicate a student's development. It indicates the strategies a student is using for spelling and whether a child can recognise a word in its conventional form. For example, in the example shown in Figure 15.16 the child who did the proofreading has found some of the original writer's errors and corrected them, and missed one or two ('poot', 'sed'). While she has recognised that 'sed' is not conventional, she hasn't quite got it under control yet ('sead'). However, the attempt 'sead' indicates that she does know that the 'ea' digraph also carries the sound that 'ai' carries in 'said'.

BE – A – DETECTIVE

Name Justin   Date 5·4·93

The Kick-a-lot Shoes.

"I want to be mean. Very, very mean. Wot can I do?" sed the wich.

She looked down at the town, "I'll kik people so hard, thay carnt sit down." she poot on her mean old kick-a-lot shoos. "Here I came, all you people"

Can you find ?

Figure 5.16: Proofreading example

57

Sharing circle field notes

Most of my personal learning about the identification and awareness of the markers of language development has come from the sharing circle which concludes the writing time. The field notes I take become the basis for what I share with the students in the sharing circle. Figure 5.17 shows a sample of the field notes I take.

SHARING CIRCLE (Field Notes for Sharing With Students)
Alan points. Read list of words. Reinforced.
Brendan. Copied my demonstration
• 2 finger test
Reinforced spaces between words.
Cherie scrounged her own word 'birthday'.
Reinforced scrounging for words
• Adding to work
Chris 't' Brendan helped him come up with teradactile
Casey Not on topic. 2 sentences.
Shaun
Raiya
◦ Upper case for name
◦ Word out of writing box. Use again.
◦ Loud voice
Stacey Writing about frogs
Kathy
Elye
Aimee Shy
Stephen
Annette working at desk
Erin at desk
Ricky at desk
Ian at desk
Stewart
Annette has drawn a 'cake', says she is going to write but adds
another

Figure 5.17: A sample of my field notes

Field notes like these have enabled me to develop a set of markers/ indicators that focus my assessment during writing time and which give me a framework for sharing my notes with the children during sharing time. Figure 5.18 shows a sample of the indicators I have managed to develop.

This activity provides me with the opportunity to observe and interact with students as they read, discuss and share their work. This is an encouraging time, a supportive time when students themselves provide excellent role models and we can celebrate and reinforce learning that I see taking place.

SHARING CIRCLE AFTER WRITING K/1.2 25/8
This is a set of indicators/markers that tell me about growth:
- *Is willing to sit in circle*
- *Is willing to share work in circle*
- *Shares audibly*
- *Uses book language when sharing text*
- *Points to words – runs finger along*
  - *– runs L→R*
  - *– points to individual words*
- *When 'reading', realises language and text does/doesn't match*
- *Writes text with matching illustration*
- *Selects words from environmental print*
- *Writes meaningful text*
- *Wishes to publish*
- *Is willing to continue writing on a piece*
- *Is having a go at spelling — initial letters match sound*

Markers which may show engagement in this activity:
- *Listens attentively*
- *Helps others read*
- *Asks questions about the piece*
- *Provides ideas*

Figure 5.18: Indicators/markers I look for during writing time

WHERE TO NEXT?

Since the beginning of the project, each subsequent year has brought new insights. Classes change and new students and new environments bring challenges which refine my practice. Presently I am looking forward to working with students in upper primary years, exploring how the children themselves can become more involved in their assessment. I believe this has great potential for empowering students in later years of secondary and tertiary education.

Over the last few years I have come to understand that I only see what I know. The cues of development have always been there. They are realities; however, it took me the process of co-researching to really see them. I found that when two people are watching the same things, the subsequent discussions about the data challenges an articulation and confirmation of what those cues of development are, especially in the light of the mandated profiles we are expected to use as a framework of student achievement.

One overarching principle which is extremely important is this: both teacher and students must be prepared to become learners, take risks, be ready to make mistakes, but also celebrate successes. Therefore a relationship of trust and a shared understanding of the purpose of learning is essential.

Organising the classroom for responsive evaluation

Pushing ahead in Years 3-6

by Nyla Simms

In Chapter 5 Janelle Graham described how she approached the task of organising her kindergarten classroom so that she could implement responsive evaluation. From the perspective of a teacher who had just begun the journey, she provided us with examples of 'how to recognise beliefs in practice', of using 'episodes' to help 'observe learners' responses', the of her 'procedures for recording information'.

In this chapter, Nyla Simms gives us the perspective of an experienced primary grades (3-6) specialist who has already begun her journey to responsive evaluation. She has strong beliefs about including parents and children in the assessment and evaluation process, and she explores another part of the conceptual map, 'reporting to audiences'.

BACKGROUND: BEFORE RESPONSIVE EVALUATION

Twice a year, at report-writing time, for most of my teaching career, I would sit alone with the blank report form in front of me and try to dredge up from my memory knowledge about each student in my care. It was a time-consuming task which usually produced some very succinct, truthful statements about the children at the 'top' and 'bottom' of the class. It was easy to write about them because they displayed obvious characteristics of academic progress and had clearly identifiable attitudes towards learning. The problem was with 'the others', that 'middle' group in every class. How did I differentiate their learning? How did I describe what they knew, what they needed to learn, what they felt about themselves as learners? In my ignorance, I clutched on to general, non-critical statements — 'progressing well', 'working to his ability', 'neat handwriting', 'careful attention to all work'. These were repeated on many reports. Poor parents! Poor children! What did those comments really mean? How did they tell the parents what the students knew and what, if any, problems they were facing?

Fortunately this has begun to change. Through professional reading over the last ten years, and through working as a co-researcher with enlightened colleagues, I have come to realise that there are many people who want or need to know about students' learning, including the parents, the teacher, the principal, grandparents and other relatives, the teacher next year, and, especially, the children. These stakeholders change during the students' lives but there are three that stay constant:

- the children
- the parents
- the teacher

I realised that there was a more comprehensive form of reporting that I could try out in my classroom. I saw how the teachers at a nearby school organised what they called 'focused evaluation' (Woodward 1992). I read about student-led conferences, learning journals, anecdotal records and portfolios. Slowly combining them over the years has led to the responsive evaluation that I use in my classroom today.

MY BELIEFS

Like Vonne Mathie (Chapter 4) I had to go through the process of making my beliefs explicit. Because my beliefs about children's learning, language, teaching, and literacy are so closely connected to my beliefs about assessment and evaluation, it is necessary to describe them briefly before getting down to the nitty-gritty of how I organise myself and my classroom for responsive evaluation. There are two aspects:

- the role of teachers, parents and children in the evaluation process
- the nature of integrated learning

The role of teachers, parents and children

I used to believe that the teacher had the major role to play in evaluating learning, that he or she was the major source of information that was ultimately evaluated. Now I believe that there are other sources of valuable information that should be incorporated into the evaluation process. I strongly believe that evaluation should be a three-way process between children, teacher and parents.

The role of children

It is important for children to have input into any evaluation of their learning. They should be encouraged to contribute to any oral or written evaluative report made on them. Why? Simply because they know a lot about their strengths and weaknesses. Teachers can encourage such self-evaluation by providing time for journal keeping, portfolio building and discussion. This process is facilitated when, as part of normal every day practice, children are informed of the purpose for any activity they are asked to do and given opportunities to reflect on the successes or failures in achieving such purposes. Students have the right to know the particular standards we use to evaluate their learning.

The role of parents

Parents know a lot about their children. They spend many hours with them engaged in a variety of activities in different environments and situations. Most parents are able and willing to share this valuable knowledge. I believe that they should also be made aware that teachers value this knowledge and need access to it.

Teachers also need to be aware of physical, medical, and personal matters that may affect children's learning and if we don't ask, sometimes we never find out.

Children need to be aware of their parents' expectations because it helps them understand what their parents value about school and learning. Children also need to be aware that their parents know about the learning programs and processes that are valued in their classroom.

I find that all this parental knowledge helps me design my learning program with more confidence so that I can meet the individual needs of each of my students.

The role of teachers

Teachers bring a professional educator's knowledge to the evaluation of each student. They determine the desired outcomes, they design the learning activities, and they plan the strategies for implementing the curriculum. It is their task to track those outcomes as the students work and they can draw upon suitable and relevant language to describe the strengths, advances and weaknesses of the students.

The nature of integrated learning

I believe that the most appropriate way for children to learn is through an integrated curriculum. I also believe that certain conditions of learning lie at the core of integrated learning and that an effective integrated learning environment can only function effectively if these conditions are in place.

The conditions of learning that I have identified as being important in my classroom are immersion, demonstrations, expectations, responsibility, feedback, approximations, practice and engagement. (Cambourne 1988) Each of these conditions has implications for the way I evaluate.

Immersion

Immersion in those aspects of language which form the focus for the unit creates and maintains a meaningful learning environment.

Implication for evaluation: I ensure that I keep track of the children's responses to the immersion activities, usually through anecdotal records.

Demonstration

Demonstrations ensure that children learn by watching and listening, then talking and doing. Demonstrations can be, and often are, incidental, but should be consciously programmed in response to identified needs.

Implication for evaluation: I record children's interest in and responses to demonstrations using checklists or anecdotal notes.

Expectations

Expectations are conveyed by the way the teacher acts, talks and behaves. Realistic expectations make success possible for each and every student.

Implication for evaluation: These expectations come from all stakeholders (the children included) and are modified according to the desired outcomes of the teaching/learning activities, the health and emotions of the children, the identified needs of the children, the latest learning the children have done, and their perceptions of their needs/directions for further learning.

Responsibility

Responsibility is an integral part of the transformation to independence in learning. Learning is a problem-solving exercise that occurs best when learners are provided with opportunities to make decisions about what they will next master.

Implication for evaluation: Each time the children are involved in these exercises, I try to be vigilant in recording decisions made and the way in which the children carried out their tasks.

Engagement

Learners can only learn from demonstrations if they engage with them. Engagement is the outcome of all these conditions working together.

Implication for evaluation: I am continually looking for what I call 'engagement cues', that is, signs that indicate that learners are engaging with the demonstrations I am providing.

Feedback

Feedback involves evaluation. Effective feedback requires an intimate knowledge of individual students and their needs. Students should be encouraged at all stages of the learning process to discuss their own efforts and the efforts of others in a constructive manner.

Implication for evaluation: One way of recording these thoughts is through the children's daily learning journal entries which become part of the overall assessment records. My anecdotal records also keep track of the children's comments and attitudes.

Approximations

Approximations are attempts to learn and children should be encouraged to 'have-a-go' at learning. They should be encouraged to reflect on their approximations as part of the evaluation process.

Implication for evaluation: Children can keep track of themselves by recording their progress in their learning journals.

Practice

Practice is essential in every learning situation. Students need to practise skills or techniques and employ knowledge, concepts and understandings. Learners need positive feedback in order to realise the significance of practice.

Implication for evaluation: Keeping checklists about the completion of tasks and recording the merit cards issued or special comments made on children's work are methods of record keeping that are easily gathered together and collated at a later date for report writing or interviews.

ORGANISING FOR RESPONSIVE EVALUATION

Identifying and opening up episodes

I chose the first two hours each morning for my language session because it sets up a routine for every day and cashes in on 'prime learning time'.

My episodes

Whole class focus	20 mins
Workshop	80 mins
Sharing	10 mins
Learning journal entries	10 mins

The sustained silent reading session is organised after the lunchbreak, with 20 minutes allocated for reading and 10 minutes for sharing.

The episodes are made up of the following possibilities depending on the time of year, the interests and needs of the students and the skills, knowledge and understandings being developed at that time.

Whole class focus

(a) I focus the students' attention on tasks, events and organisational matters.

(b) I read to the class — this may be the text for class study, it may be for the study of a particular genre. It may relate to our author study.

(c) I write in front of the students as I do a think-aloud to demonstrate a point about the writing process.

OR I demonstrate how new language activities are done, e,g., a sociogram, a story ladder, planning a character for a narrative, planning the plot for a narrative, organising a report;

OR I focus on a student's piece of work to demonstrate and clarify parts of the writing process that have been identified as a need within the class;

OR I focus on particular skills of spelling, grammar and handwriting;

OR I focus on the assigned activity and the expectations I have about organising, researching, drafting, conferencing and presenting the work;

OR I focus on what criteria students should employ when choosing work to store in their portfolios;

OR I focus on a genre and, with the students, make a retrieval chart about its features so that the information can be used later.

Workshop

At the beginning of the year, this is the opportunity for students to:
• write what they want
• learn about my expectations of them as writers:
    Do they stay on task for a set period?
    Do they have a go at spelling?
    Can they proofread their drafts?
    Do they believe that they are writers?
    Do they use ideas from their own experiences or their exposure to literature etc. for their writing?
• learn about the stages of the writing process
• to build up a repertoire of written pieces that they can choose to take to publication

Later in the year, this gives students a block of time for concentration on any assigned piece of writing or a chance to experiment with writing of their own choice.

It is also an opportunity for the teacher to record anecdotal notes about each student:
• what they choose to write
• how they get on task and stay that way
• how much they understand about the stages of the writing process

- what difficulties they are experiencing
- what conventions they have control over or are developing
- features that need to become a whole class or group focus for demonstration

It is the time for teachers to observe, evaluate, interact, direct and redirect, question and refocus, clarify and analyse the students' learning and writing. This may be achieved through:

- literature-based activities e.g., reflections on the studied text, literary activities from the demonstration session;
- word puzzles and activities based on vocabulary from the studied text or other areas of the curriculum;
- a long-term assignment requiring research, planning, organisation of facts and publication. This may continue as homework and return to this time slot over several days;
- an author study activity;
- editing, conferencing and publishing an assigned or personal choice piece of writing.

The teacher's task during this episode is constant observation, evaluation, analysis and interaction.

Sharing

Students volunteer to share their work, either partly completed or in the published state, from the previous two episodes. This is an opportunity for students to seek and gain peer opinions and advice on improving the work. The teacher's task is to respond to their written texts when necessary. I make anecdotal notes which later become the basis of my focused report writing.

Learning journal entries

At first, students are asked to reflect on the morning's work and write about it, answering these questions:

> What have you learnt?
> How did you learn it?
> What did you enjoy or dislike and why?
> What would you like to improve?

By week four, the students are encouraged to make positive and negative comments about their learning, which become a vital resource when I am writing focused reports or discussing their progress with the students or parents.

Sustained silent reading and sharing

After the lunch break, the students move into the classroom, choose a book or books, or resume the book they are currently reading. They may sit at their desks or on the floor. There must be silence for the duration of the session and the teacher also reads silently.

At the end of 20 minutes, the whole class moves to the floor space and no more than four volunteers share what they have been reading. They are expected to:

- summarise the plot or content of the text
- recommend the book to a person or group and say why
- read aloud an excerpt

During this sharing, the teacher's task is to make anecdotal records. Often, I also record what each student is reading during SSR which keeps me in touch with their choices and the variety of texts being read. It also gives me a record of whether or not they have completed a text. Towards the end of term, if a student has not volunteered to share, I arrange beforehand with them that they are expected to share that day.

Organising strategies for assessment and evaluation

When I am confronted with a blank sheet of paper on which I am going to write a descriptive report, I need to have available a variety of facts about the children so that I can construct a meaningful picture of progress for the parents and children.

I need to have several forms of data collection strategies operating in my classroom so that my evaluations are reliable and relevant for the learning progress at that time.

Anecdotal records

These are single pages for each student, kept in a ring-binder. Every day, I try to note some point about each child's learning behavior, attitudes or choices. Over a period of weeks, I may record:

- book choices for SSR
- writing choices each session
- whether the student volunteers to share reading and writing
- if this sharing is interesting/competent
- which oral or written language skills the student has under control
- which oral or written skills need to be addressed
- whether these needs become an individual or small group or class focus for learning
- whether assigned work has been completed

- the degree of care in presentation and accuracy of the work
- incidental notes about health, extra-curricula interests

As these anecdotal notes build, this assessment tool can begin to drive the program of learning. Every time I make notes about the children's needs, I must then rethink the program of learning so that I can meet these needs.

As I reflect on the anecdotal notes, and program anew, I ask:

- What student assessment will happen? In groups, in journals, in pairs, talking, writing, art, retell, etc.?
- What will I use to evaluate the work?
    observation and notes
    check lists
    oral reading
    talking
    game behavior
    look at specific outcomes
    writing in journals
    general class demeanor
- What skills will be emphasised?
- What attitudes will be emphasised?
- What knowledge will be emphasised?
- Will this unit of study encourage independent learning by the nature of the activities?

Portfolios

I also negotiate the keeping of portfolios by the children so that they can collect items that reflect their learning and their pride in achievements. These manilla folders, often decorated by the children, are stored upright in a cardboard box so that chosen pieces of work can be slipped in easily. Students and teacher choose pieces that indicate growth in skills, knowledge or attitudes, and it is important that the teacher discusses the reasons for selecting a piece of work with the children.

When the piece is selected, the students write why it has been chosen on a removable sticker and attach it to the piece. This permanent reflection, written at the time, is far more meaningful for the children, parents and teacher when the time comes to summarise the learning which has occurred.

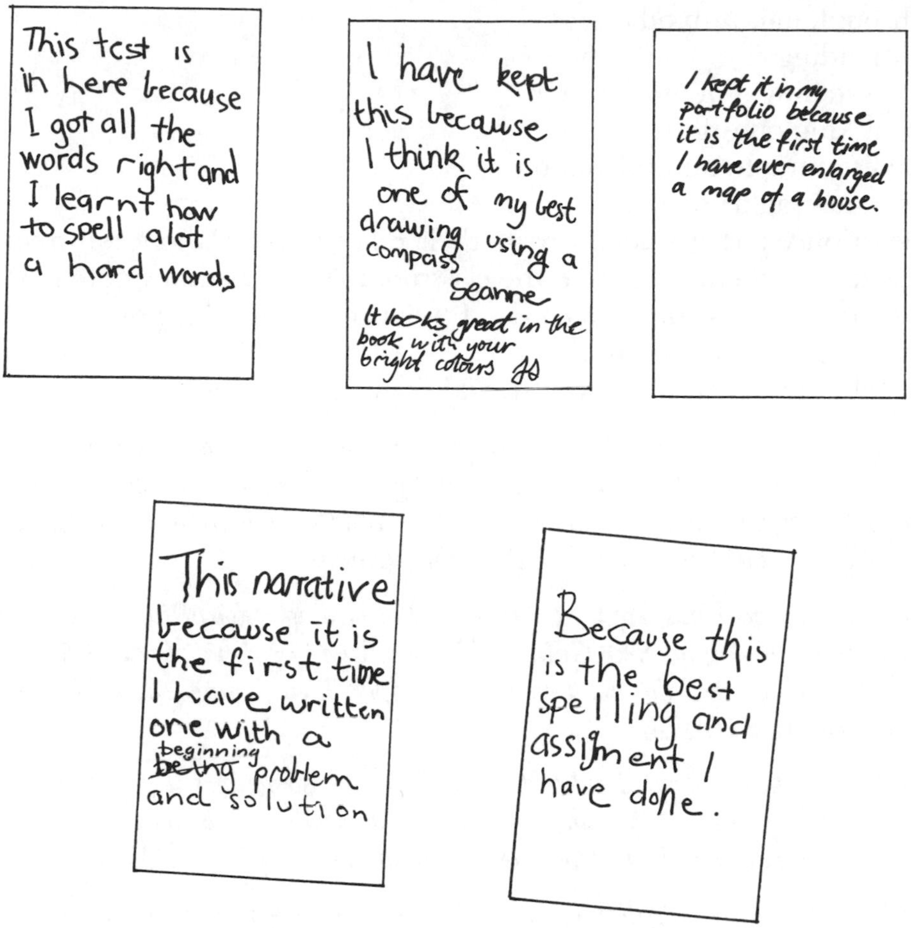

This test is in here because I got all the words right and I learnt how to spell a lot a hard words

I have kept this because I think it is one of my best drawing using a compass Seanne It looks great in the book with your bright colours 😊

I kept it in my portfolio because it is the first time I have ever enlarged a map of a house.

This narrative because it is the first time I have written one with a beginning problem and solution

Because this is the best spelling and assimment I have done.

Figure 6.1: An example of students' comments on portfolio pieces

Learning journals

Early in the teaching year, the students are introduced to learning journal writing. As each session is brought to a close, the students are asked to reflect on their learning and write about what they have learnt and how they have learnt it, any problems they have encountered and not been able to solve or how they did solve a particular problem. They are also encouraged to suggest the direction of their learning for the future. I view this activity as the major instrument through which children can inform me or the parents about their learning.

I try to encourage oral reflection as well as this written reflection. After many discussions and demonstrations, children begin to be able to say how they learnt a particular thing. The discussions are about how learning takes place:

through talk with others
by reading
by watching a demonstration
by asking questions
by listening to an explanation
by watching a video …

At least once a day, students write their reflections for about ten minutes. I read them as I circulate around the classroom and sometimes note particular insights in the anecdotal records. I refer to them during the year for interviews and report writing.

The following examples show the wide range of possibilities.

What I think Terabithia has done to Jesse is put spirit in him and made him have confidence. He thought he couldn't do anything before but now he can. When Leslie died he took it as a grown-up. After a while he started to be more responsible. He cared for Maybelle and put her as queen of Terabithia. (Ahmed)

Thank you for teaching me well this term. I'm having a lot of fun in your class. I like learning about Papua New Guinea. I have a friend in Wombat called Ari. She has a sister called Cisca and they both come from Papua New Guinea. Now I know more about their country. (Jessica)

I don't really think about 'Bridge To Terabithia' but sometimes it pops up sad in my mind. I did a big plan for my narrative and it makes it easy to write. I think it will turn out not too bad then I can type it on my computer and print it. (Miodrag)

I have been reading thriller books and it is really improving my reading. I like writing the narrative. I would like to spell correctly the first time I write a word. I dislike not being able to use my PURPLE PEN! (Natalie)

We have been writing a narrative. First we planned things about the characters and the plot. Then we started writing the draft using the plans. I have nearly finished mine. I think it might have eight chapters. (Dannielle)

Parent meetings

Before the end of the third week in Term One, a meeting is arranged with all parents. This is an opportunity for us to get to know each other. It also gives me the chance to:
• impart my expectations of behavior and work habits
• inform about planned units of study, special activities, organisation of duties
• introduce focused evaluation and reports
• explain the 'triangle of assessment' (teacher-parent-child)

- explain the use of the student's learning journal
- explain the parent observation sessions
- answer questions from the parents

By week 6, Term One, parents receive letters to:

- introduce focused evaluation
- request completion of the parent response sheet
- request a booking for parent observation sessions (3 choices)
- present the set of observation questions

Figure 6.2: Letter to parents

GWYNNEVILLE PUBLIC SCHOOL

11 March 1993

Dear Parents

FOCUSED EVALUATION

Class 5/6 will be assessed in three ways this year:

- by themselves
- by the teacher
- by their parent(s)

My program is to write two focused reports for each child by the middle of Term Three.

I would also like parents to do two things:

(1) Complete the Parent Response Sheet and return it to school as soon as possible.

(2) Visit our classroom. You will spend 40 minutes observing your child in the learning situation and answer the observation questions which are included with this letter. Your child will then spend the next 40 minutes showing and explaining to you the importance of the work we have done and collected in his/her portfolio.

The children are assessing themselves through entries in their Learning Journals and the discussions in group work.

By mid-Term Three you and your child will, if you wish, be invited to an interview with me. More about that later in the year.

As is customary, you will receive a summative report during Term 4. The times available for you to visit the classroom are 9.30am – 11.00am on the following dates. Please fill in the attached form to indicate your preferences for dates you can attend.

Monday March 15	Tuesday April 6	Tuesday June 22
Tuesday March 16	Tuesday June 1	Tuesday July 13
Thursday March 18	Thursday June 3	Thursday July 15
Monday March 22	Monday June 7	Monday July 19
Tuesday March 23	Tuesday June 8	Monday July 26

Thursday March 25 | Thursday June 10 | Thursday July 29
Monday March 29 | Monday June 14 | Monday August 2
Thursday April 1 | Thursday June 17 | Tuesday August 3
Monday April 5 | Monday June 21

Parent Response Sheet

Dear Teacher

Thank you for helping me to look closely at _____ reading and writing. These are some of the other things I have noticed about him/her at home:

Regards..

MY CHILD AS A READER

Please indicate your observations of your child's reading at home.

My child selects books that are suitable for him/her

My child reads to me

My child attempts to read in everyday situations (e.g. signs, magazines, labels, etc.)

My child can retell so that I can understand

My child likes me to read to him/her

My child is willing to take a guess at unknown words or attempts to figure them out

My child figures out new words he/she sees by:

    Looking at the pictures

    Listening to what the text has been about, rereading and taking a guess

    Sounding out the word

My child is able to tell me about what he/she has read

MY CHILD AS A WRITER

Please indicate your observations of your child's writing at home.

My child enjoys writing in his/her leisure time

My child likes to talk about or display his/her writing

My child uses writing to send messages to others

My child writes in different ways (e.g. messages, stories, poems, letters)

My child can:
(a) write a draft
(b) check the spelling
(c) check the draft is punctuated correctly

My child's writing makes sense

My child will try out new words on his/her own then check with a dictionary

My child usually likes to write about:

MY CHILD AND SCHOOL

My child enjoys going to school

My child likes to talk about things that happen at school

My child plays well both as an individual and in a group

My child readily accepts responsibility

My child is organised:
    has a set time for watching TV, play, bed, reading
    delivers notes and returns them to school if necessary
    knows when library books are due
    knows when homework or assignments are due
    brings notes when absent

My child asks me for help when in difficulty

My child is a member of and uses the local library

My child's out-of-school activities are:

_____

_____

Focused evaluation

While we wait for the parent response sheets to be returned, I help the students prepare their report folders. In class, and at my home, the report folders are prepared in the following way:

- students draw a self-portrait
- manila folders are halved
- folders are labelled with names
- returned parent observations sheets are attached
- report sheets are attached

During the week in every language session, I focus on four students noting:

- behavior and work in each episode
- perceived needs
- interaction with peers
- attitudes
- skill and concept development

The report is written at the weekend and sent home the following Monday with a parent–child response sheet attached.

This routine is repeated over 7–8 weeks until all students have received one report. For the second round of reports, I focus on all curriculum areas.

The actual collection of information during the focus time has presented difficulties and I am still altering, refining and experimenting with ways of making the writing time more manageable. I tried carrying a folder around with me as I circulated around the classroom but I kept losing it as I put it down when I helped children, then not much was written about the focus students. I also tried attaching sheets of paper to the focus children's desks and writing about them as I passed their desks. At present I use a pocket note-book and write in a form of shorthand. I do have to reread the notes on a daily basis to translate my shorthand for future understanding. The other difficulty is finding the time in a busy classroom to keep notes. Some days, the development of activities may mean I don't write anything during class time but I have to be vigilant and spend break times catching up with the note-making.

I would like to include the other children in this and give them the opportunity to add their knowledge about their peers. I may be able to combine my pocket notebook with the paper on the desks for the other children to write on.

Responsive evaluation overview

For 1993, this was my planned overview of evaluation commitments. It helps to set them out like this so that the interruptions are part of the plan — long-service leave, dance festival, choral festival, special days, etc.

Term One
Week 3
Parent meeting — offer explanations of the focus week for the students, parent response sheet and observation booking sheet. Answer questions about evaluation.

Week 6, 7, 8, 9
Focus on four students per week and write reports.
Arrange parent observations two days each week.

Term Two
Weeks 1-6
On leave.

Weeks 7, 8, 9
Focus on four students per week and write reports.
Arrange parent observations two days each week.
(Total 28 reports)
(Total 14 parent observations)

Term Three
Weeks 1-7
• Focus on four students each week and write their second reports.
• Two parent observations each week.
(Total 28 reports)
(Total 14 parent observations)

Week 8
Parent–child–teacher interviews for all students.
15–20 minutes allocated per student.

Term Four
School report forms are used to write a summative report of this year's progress for every student.

Focused evaluation reports

The four focused reports usually take me about three hours' work during the weekend. I find it easier to gather my thoughts and write away from the hustle and bustle and interruptions of the classroom. I can be certain of a quiet block of time each Sunday and a day's rest allows me to think about my writing and what I have learnt about the children.

In the long term, this organisation lessens the stress of writing thirty half-yearly reports over one week. I gather together my anecdotal records, focus notes, the student's learning journals and the parent response sheets. If parents have visited the classroom and responded to the observation questions, these are also consulted.

With all this data in front of me, I must determine the form my writing will take. I base each comment on the episodes of each day.

Also, as part of my programming, I plan certain evaluation activities or products. They are put into the overview. This is the overview for Terms One and Two 1993.

STUDENT EVALUATION OVERVIEW CLASS 5/6

TERM ONE
Week 1   Observation (ongoing)
Week 2   Anecdotal records ... learning journals (ongoing)
Week 3   Focusing and reporting ... literature retell
Week 4   ... Maths mentals test
Week 5   ... Writing work sample collected
Week 6   ... Proofreading activity
Week 7   ... Peer spelling tests
Week 8
Week 9   ... Narrative published
Week 10 ... Spelling word puzzles

TERM TWO
Week 1   ... Space quiz
Week 2   ... Readers theatre participation
Week 3   ... Cloze activity 'Space'
Week 4   ... Homework assignment
Week 5   ... Handwriting ... speech marks ... maths test ... 'Feelings' cloze
Week 6   ... Writing product evaluation
Week 7   ... Maths retelling
Week 8   ... Relationships perceptions
Week 9
Week 10 ... Child protection concepts and understandings

The focused evaluation report takes shape with data from:
- learning journals
- anecdotal records
- focused evaluation notes
- product evaluations
- results of class activities and book work

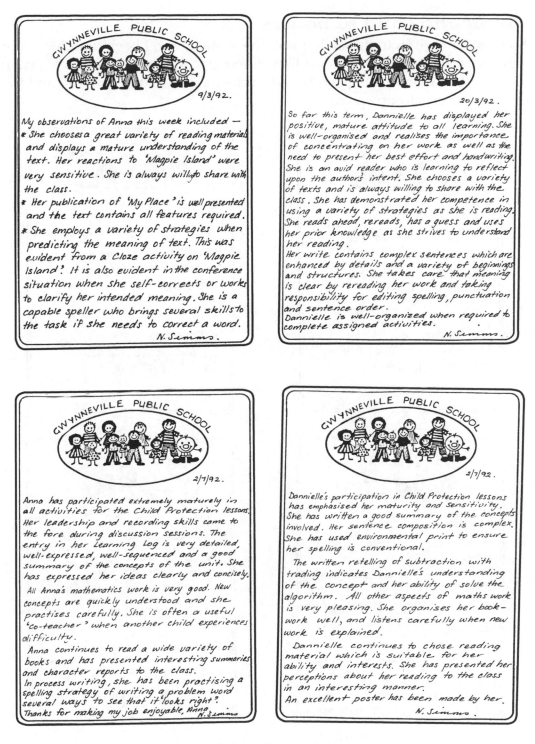

Figure 6.3: An example of student reports

Parent and child responses

This report is given to the students on the Monday and I begin another set of four focused evaluation notes on four different students for that week. When the reports go home, the parents and student are invited to respond and the invitation is usually accepted.

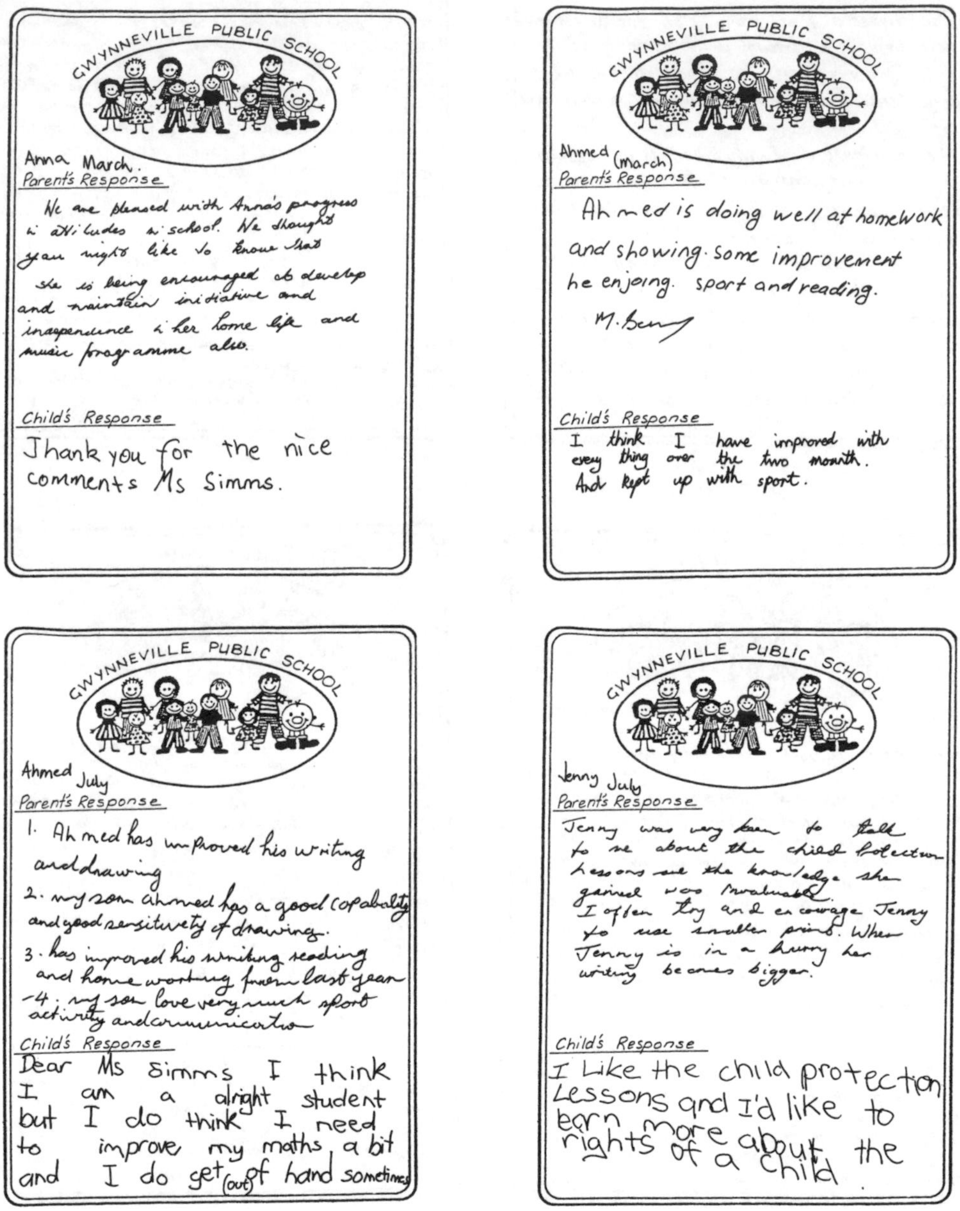

GWYNNEVILLE PUBLIC SCHOOL

Anna March.
Parent's Response

We are pleased with Anna's progress in attitudes in school. We thought you might like to know that she is being encouraged to develop and maintain initiative and independence in her home life and music programme also.

Child's Response

Thank you for the nice comments Ms Simms.

GWYNNEVILLE PUBLIC SCHOOL

Ahmed (march)
Parent's Response

Ahmed is doing well at homework and showing some improvement he enjoing. sport and reading.

M. Berry

Child's Response

I think I have improved with every thing over the two month. And kept up with sport.

GWYNNEVILLE PUBLIC SCHOOL

Ahmed July
Parent's Response

1. Ahmed has improved his writing and drawing

2. my son ahmed has a good copabality and good sensitivity of drawing.

3. has improved his writing reading and home working from last year

4. my son love very much sport activity and communication

Child's Response

Dear Ms Simms I think I am a alright student but I do think I need to improve my maths, a bit and I do get (out) of hand sometimes

---

GWYNNEVILLE PUBLIC SCHOOL

Jenny July
Parent's Response

Jenny was very keen to talk to me about the child Protection Lessons and the knowledge she gained was invaluable. I often try and encourage Jenny to use smaller print. When Jenny is in a hurry her writing becomes bigger.

Child's Response

I Like the child protection Lessons and I'd like to earn more about the rights of a child.

Figure 6.4: Some responses

Parent observation

By mid-March, the parents have begun to book in a time for observation in the class. During their visit, they are asked to observe their child and respond to the questions on the observation sheet.

QUESTIONS	YOUR COMMENTS
How does your child interact with others? What does he/she do during • group work, • whole class activity, • individual work?	
What is his/her attitude to class work? Does he/she seem to enjoy what he/she is doing? Does he/she have difficulty settling down to the task at hand?	
What surprises have you discovered about your child?	
What is something special that you have noticed about him/her today?	
How does he/she solve any problems that may have arisen?	
What decisions did he/she make today? How easy was it for him/her to make those decisions?	
What have you noticed at home that your child can do which he/she has not displayed during today's session?	
	Signed _____(Parent)

Figure 6.5: Observation sheet

These questions help the parent to focus on their own child and provide a framework for writing about their child. The observation usually lasts about forty minutes, then the children take their parents on to the verandah and explain their portfolio collection and the reasons that certain pieces have been included. This is followed by a three-way discussion over morning tea which gives the children and parents the opportunity to clarify what has occurred.

I usually share my anecdotal records at that time and explain the way in which I may analyse the results of the morning's activities, the entries in the learning journal and my focused evaluation notes.

Parent responses

Anna

Cooperative. Self-motivated.

Competent. Independent. Accepts the idea of the task as a natural part of life and performs without hesitation. I note that Anna and all other children don't know where the 'Far East' is. Do they know the 'Middle East' — a term in current use in view of the USA/Israeli/ Arab conflicts. Anna takes 'being a student' very seriously and will not, even for a second, contemplate 'being a daughter' in the class context. She treats her peers with consideration — no rushing in — never claims to know something she doesn't BUT equally doesn't push knowledge forward. What surprises? How remarkably like her Dad's responses and work habits Anna's are!!

Brooke

Brooke listens. She seems reluctant to answer questions and I'm sure she knows the answer. She interacts well with her group, asking what they think and putting her views in as well. Her attitude to her work is very positive. She really wants to do her best but she seems to need reassurance from her group. She settled down and got the job done, even though there was lots of activity around her. At home it takes a real effort to get her to do that. Maybe because I was watching her?

Liana

Interacts with others – Fine.

Individual work – Pen to paper immediately.

Attitude to class work – Loves class work and enjoys what she is doing. Maths was a great problem. Liana is more interested in the subject now. I am very surprised with Liana's attitude towards her work. An incredible change this year. Problems are solved either by asking the teacher or a student.

Dany

Dany and his group work together and they discuss the problem nicely. He tries to finish all his work. He seems to enjoy the work, particularly in the group activities. I think Dany is strong in mathematics but not in making an essay. He has to improve more in writing and spelling. He always asks his group if he can't solve the problem.

The second series of focused evaluation reports are planned to cover all curriculum areas and should be presented to parents during Term Three. There is also a parent–child–teacher meeting organised for the latter part of Term Three during which stakeholders can share the progress to date. I usually allocate 15–20 minutes per student for this discussion. The child is able to share work I have collected with the parent such as writing product, evaluations, maths tests, samples of the child's handwriting and drafting, records of their reading, records of completion of work and my anecdotal records.

School summative report

School policy dictates the completion of an end-of-year summative report for each student. This is sent to parents in the latter part of Term Four. Because of the year's communications I'm more comfortable in writing this report. I have much data about the children and know that the report reflects a sound knowledge of the progress and needs of the children in my care. I feel particularly confident now being able to report using the outcomes in the outcomes standards framework which is in the mandatory English K-6 syllabus.

WHERE DO I GO NOW?

This is where I have arrived at the time of writing, and I need to determine my course of action for the future. I am pleased that this form of assessment and report writing has improved my knowledge about those children in the 'middle' of the class. It has meant I am more confident when I write comments about the children because I know I have plenty of data to support my words. I am becoming more aware of the power of language in describing the children and letting their comments flavor mine instead of grasping for cliches or generalisations to describe their progress and needs.

I know I need to be more vigilant in keeping anecdotal records and recording my knowledge of each student. I do want to streamline the keeping of records and intend experimenting with a personal journal which I will write at the same time every day. This could even replace the anecdotal records folder. For me, the best time to write will be immediately after the children have left the classroom at the end of the day.

I would like to streamline the correspondences with parents and design a more comprehensive questionnaire for them. The way in which the children build their portfolios needs improvement and I need to allocate more time each day for learning journal writing.

This process of assessment and reporting will never be perfect and will need to be adapted as each class demands, but I feel confident that I am not only reporting adequately to parents about their children's achievements, but also using the data collected to develop teaching and learning experiences that further enhance my students' learning.

7

Children as evaluators

Understanding evaluation from the inside

by Maxine Green

Maxine Green is a practising classroom teacher who adopts a slightly different stance. She believes that students should understand evaluation from the inside, and that when this happens it becomes much more meaningful to them and works better. She also had another agenda: her students would be entering the secondary school system in the following year where they would be subjected to numerical marks, grades, and scores, and she felt if they understood some of the underlying principles they would be better placed to cope.
In this chapter she describes how she and another teacher teamed to help a double class of Year 6 children become better informed about the evaluation of their learning.
She describes the way she and her team partner designed and taught some language units specifically aimed to help their students examine and unpack the assessment and evaluation process, question it, and confront many of the issues that evaluators typically have to solve.

BACKGROUND

In 1991 I team taught a Year 6 at Warrawong Primary School (NSW) with Vicki Moses. We were responsible for 57 children. For many years Warrawong had relied on a predominantly qualitative approach to evaluation. In hindsight, we realise that we had been practising our own version of responsive evaluation.

We were concerned that when our sixth grade children proceeded to the local high school they would be faced with a system of evaluation predominantly based on numerical scores and grades, and that after six years of qualitative evaluation many of them would find this confusing and difficult. Therefore we planned some language units to help them understand evaluation at a deeper level.

We believed that learners who are metacognitively aware of how something like evaluation 'works' (know it from the inside) are better positioned to confront, challenge and negotiate their way around confusions and perceived injustices.

There were 57 students in the class, 32 girls and 25 boys. Warrawong is a multi-ethnic school. Most of the students come from non-English speaking backgrounds (NESB). At the time of this project there were 28 different language groups within the school. Only 4% of the total enrolment of 546 were English-speaking background (ESB) children. In this grade the level of proficiency in English ranged from first phase learners to third phase learners. A whole-learning philosophy with a strong functional linguistic view of language drove the language curriculum. Most of these Year 6 children had been in the school since Kindergarten, and were accustomed to teaching practices that reflected these philosophies. The school had also been working on an approach to assessment and evaluation that reflected these models of learning and language. Staff had devised a 'product-process' model of assessment and evaluation with a reporting system based on parent–child–teacher–interpreter interviews.

Both of us believed strongly in the principles behind whole-learning (Cambourne 1988, 1992; Cordeiro 1992; Holdaway 1974) and Vicki and I had a set of beliefs about classroom practice based on these principles. These beliefs were:
- it is crucial to make the purposes of classroom practices explicit
- reflection on one's own learning is important in order to develop control of knowledge, understanding and skills
- learners should be provided with opportunities to talk their way to meaning — discussion is essential for effective learning
- sharing is one of the most powerful learning strategies available
- probing questions that force the learner to strip away the surface layer to reach that deeper level of understanding are crucial for helping students make the important connections
- co-operation and collaboration enhance learning
- shared celebration of the success of self and others is crucial to the development of a collegial and collaborative learning environment
- modelling and good demonstrations are at the core of effective teaching
- learners must develop ownership and take responsibility for the learning process

- all members of a learning community must:
  - develop a mutual trust
  - become risk takers
  - operate within the constraints exerted by external forces

THE BIG PICTURE

This project was motivated by several factors.

- We wanted our students to understand that:
  - assessment and evaluation were integral parts of the learning process
  - assessment and evaluation were not add-ons that came at the end of a unit
  - assessment and evaluation were necessary to direct further learning
- We were convinced that:
  - when students acquired these understandings they would assume more responsibility and control of their learning
  - students learn better when in a co-learning relationship

Co-learning makes it difficult to plan the project within a predetermined time frame because the children have to steer the process. This meant that the project unfolded as the community of learners in the classroom worked through it.

We then developed this set of outcomes:

Students will:

- learn to reflect on their own learning
- learn how to use a reflective learning journal
- use their entries in these journals as 'data' about their learning
- learn how to interpret (analyse) these data
- learn how to set goals/action plans based on these data
- understand the issues in reporting the interpretations to another audience, in this case parents.

Then we divided the project into two very broad components:

1. Learning self-evaluation
2. Learning peer evaluation

Learning self-evaluation

We decided that a unit on self-evaluation would be a good way to achieve most of the outcomes listed above.

Learning peer evaluation

As we reflected more deeply we realised that there were some other outcomes which self evaluation would achieve:

Students will:

- develop markers of evaluation
- recognise these when they occur
- interpret what these markers mean
- explore options for presenting results (grades, scores, samples, narratives)

We decided that a unit on peer evaluation would achieve these outcomes if it built on those developed through the self-evaluation unit.

We didn't set a time frame for these two components. We wanted our students to learn to take some responsibility for when and how the concepts we hoped to achieve in each component would be taught and learned and we wanted to let them experience the power of shared decision-making and shared meaning. The project unfolded as we addressed the issues and concerns we encountered in each component. As it turned out, the self-evaluation component was completed between weeks 3-9 in Term One and the unit on peer evaluation completed between weeks 3-9 in Term Two.

THE NITTY-GRITTY

We began by sharing our agenda at a class discussion session and posing these questions:

- What do you think we mean by the words assessment and evaluation?
- How do we (teachers) assess and evaluate your development at school?
- Why do you think we assess and evaluate you?

We believed it was crucial to make the purposes of classroom practices explicit, so we weren't surprised when the children were able to give quite comprehensive responses to these questions. Not only were they aware of the range of assessment strategies that we employed but had also helped us in the past. The list they brainstormed included:

- product evaluations
- retellings
- anecdotal records
- observations
- conferencing
- sharing sessions

We then asked them to reflect on the following question:

- Who else could assess and evaluate you?

Their suggestions included:

- other teachers
- parents
- family members
- friends
- themselves

As a whole class we discussed the concept of self-assessment more fully, examining some strategies and structures that we could use to implement it. At the conclusion of the session the children were required to make a commitment. Most were keen to become involved. Not only did the project sound exciting but we had demonstrated that we valued their input, participation and contribution and were willing to share this assessment responsibility with them. In other words, the students felt a sense of shared ownership.

During our language sessions we shared and discussed processes, product and learning connections by continually asking the group three questions:
- What did you do during the language session?
- What did you learn?
- How did you learn it?

We found it crucial to pose other probing questions that would force our learners to strip away the surface answers they made in order to reach a deeper level where learning connections are made. After sharing their thoughts in sharing time, they were invited to write independently in their learning journals for 5–10 minutes. Later they were invited to share these reflections with a partner or small group.

As well, the students used their learning journals to collect personal data and record individual connections. Often they were asked to respond to specific focus questions designed to create a mindset for later discussion.

Example 1: Vicki and I believe that co-operation and collaboration enhance learning. Therefore we planned specific learning experiences to develop the skills and understandings necessary to participate in co-operative learning. At the conclusion of one such activity we asked the children to reflect on their experiences and record what the main learning points were for them. The focus question was 'What are the qualities of a good group leader?'

> Today I learnt lots about group work. I learnt that being a group leader you don't boss people around. You be part of the group. You must co-operate.

Not only was Ahmet's reflection a personal record of his own learning, but when shared among his peers, it provided a point for later thought and discussion.

Example 2: The use of reflection and journal writing also helped to solve classroom problems. We recognised that a number of children were experiencing difficulties 'settling down' during our sustained silent reading episode and posed the following questions for reflection.

• Why do we participate in SSR?
• What do you learn during this time?
• How can we improve SSR for everyone?

Ahmet wrote:

> Sighlent Reading   28 May
>
> Today I learnt that reading warms up my brain. I think that people don't read because they aren't organised. I love reading, sometimes I get very annoyed when people around me talk when I read, then I don't learn when I read, neither do the people that are talking.

During a whole group sharing session this independent reflection, together with other data, led to the formulation of new 'ground rules' for our SSR episode. We continued to monitor and refine SSR using this strategy.

The children's learning journals became a prime source of rich and authentic data which, over time, clearly demonstrated the development of understandings, concepts and connections. Vicki and I used this data to supplement and verify what we'd collected through observation, conferencing, sharing, sampling, and retelling. It also helped us to make programming decisions.

We encouraged the children to review their own data in order to recognise their own (and their peers') growth and development. The shared celebration of their successes was crucial to the development of a collegial and collaborative learning environment. Children frequently burst into impromptu applause when their peers shared the success stories they recorded in their journals.

Using journals to establish learning goals and action plans

The children also regularly used their journal records to help them formulate new learning goals. We first demonstrated this task by collaboratively constructing a response to the instruction:

'Consider the modes of language learning — reading, writing, talking, listening, spelling and handwriting — and decide on a specific area in which you would like to make improvement/s'.

We collated responses on chart paper and explained how we would use them to help us design our teaching/learning programs. We then selected the most common response and discussed the concept of goal setting and the formulation of an action plan. The final result was displayed in the room as a model for learners to use.

Model of how to make a goal and action plan

1. Write your goal: To improve my reading skills by learning more strategies to use when I'm blocked
2. Set a date to reach your goal: Week 10 – Term Two
3. Plan three things you will do to reach your goal:
   - listen carefully during sharing time when peers discuss the various strategies they use when they are blocked
   - refer and add to the class chart 'Reading — Strategies To Use When Blocked'
   - observe a buddy read aloud and record the strategies they use when blocked — discuss later with buddy and whole class group

The children then used this model to develop their own action plan. They selected an area of personal need and a partner with similar interests, and proceeded to work through the process to complete their personal action plans. Action plans were shared and published to allow others to support and contribute to each other's learning. The children continued to collect data in their journals and at the appropriate time used this information to determine how successful they had been in reaching their stated goals. They also discussed the effectiveness of their action plans. After recording and reflecting on this information they again chose an area of need and the process began again.

Using journals to report to parents

The class began to explore the possibility of going the next step, that is, reporting our self-evaluations to parents. This seemed a natural course to pursue; if we were willing to share the responsibility of evaluation with our students, then why not share the responsibility of reporting to parents? We discussed this with the children and made decisions about:

- what would be reported
- the format of the report
- how it would be reported

What would be reported

Vicki and I both believe that attitude development is crucial to the development of effective learning practices. Therefore we decided to structure the report around attitude. We led a class discussion on the importance of attitudes and the role they played in our everyday lives. We defined attitudes as 'how we think and feel about particular things'. Because attitudes are individual and personal we decided to use self as the consistent factor when reflecting and reporting on attitudes towards others and school. The headings for this section of the report then became:

How I think and feel about ...
- myself
- myself and others
- myself and my school

The next section of the report asked the children to examine their learning in terms of newly acquired skills, knowledge, understandings and concepts. We did not expect the children's responses to address all aspects of learning. Our intention was to provide enough scope for all to respond in a manner that demonstrated that growth and development had taken place within and across curriculum area/s. We also wanted the children to identify and report on the direction their learning should take. We decided that they should respond to these headings:

- I have learnt how to ...
- I would like to learn more about ...
- I have enjoyed ...

The final section of the report was to be the responsibility of the teachers. This was our opportunity to reflect on the extensive data we had collected and to provide the parents with written feedback on children's learning. It is important to mention that at the time our school policy did not include a written form of reporting to parents, because a high percentage of our parents were from non-English speaking backgrounds and consequently found that written reports offered them very little in the way of meaningful information. The school had sought to meet this parental need by offering three parent–teacher meetings throughout the year and relied heavily on the assistance of interpreters to provide information to both parties. Over a period of time, changes in our parent/community composition led to a change in needs and a number of parents began to request written reports.

For these reasons parent and teacher interest in our co-researching project was high, and new developments were met with encouragement and support.

The format of the report

The class decided that the report should be printed on both sides of an A4 sheet. This sheet was placed 'longways' and folded in half twice over. This produced a four page report set out as follows:

Page 1: Front cover — school name, grade, title (self-evaluation), child's name, class, date

Page 2: How I think and feel about ...: myself, myself and others, myself and my school

Page 3: I have learnt how to ... and I would like to learn more about ...

Page 4: I have enjoyed ..., and teacher comments

The children produced a draft report and enlisted the assistance of a computer expert (the principal) who formated and printed it on laser printer. The finished product looked very professional.

How the report would be delivered

After deciding on *what* would be reported, we developed a process for *how* it would be delivered. The class agreed that parents would be surprised and excited to receive the report at the mid-year parent/teacher meeting. They decided to conduct a three-way discussion structured in a manner that allowed each stakeholder to contribute and share information. In a nutshell, this is the process that was decided upon:

1. Children prepare own written reports
2. Children write and send a special invitation to their parents
3. Invitation to outline the organisation of the session
    Organisation:
    – teachers share their data
    – children share the information on the report
    – parents invited to respond to the data presented
    – parents offer feedback

To prepare the report, the children had to refer to their learning journals to refresh their memories, collect evidence, and look for markers of their own growth. They produced a draft that addressed the various sections of the report and conferenced with a peer. At this peer conference the children sought not only to clarify meaning and conventionalise spelling and handwriting but to add another perspective to the report. We found, for example, that students helped each other make connections about strengths each of them had that they'd overlooked. An example was Suzi, who hadn't realised that when she took a part in readers theatre she was also demonstrating understanding of the character and comprehension of the plot.

Reporting to parents: What happened

Without exception, each parent was surprised and thrilled not only to receive the report, but also to have it explained and discussed by their children in a mature and knowledgeable manner. One parent in particular expressed her feelings: 'I just didn't think … could do anything like this!' The experience had not only given the child the opportunity to grow and develop, but had also allowed the parent to see the child from another perspective and appreciate them as empowered learners. The children themselves displayed immense pride in their effort and enjoyed the feedback from their parents.

They said they felt good about themselves as learners and had more confidence in themselves and their ability to tackle new learning tasks.

FROM SELF-EVALUATION TO PEER EVALUATION

Peer evaluation further explores the concept of the nature and role of evaluation when performed by someone else. It develops an understanding of issues such as expectation, evaluation criteria, methods of providing meaningful feedback — marks, rankings, grades, comments — and the notion of the accountability of the person/s performing the assessment.

While this strategy involves all class members, its success depends on a sub-group who become a peer evaluation panel with the role of evaluating the others in the class. Vicki and I found it necessary of to provide:

- appropriate demonstrations of what such a panel would do
- ample time for reflection, discussion and sharing
- constant reminders that the processes that fellow students used to achieve their products needed to be taken into account

The process used to get peer evaluation started

We built this project on experiences our students had in the self-evaluation project. After several months we introduced the concept of peer evaluation. Because they had been gathering information about the role and purpose of assessment and evaluation we did not need to devote as much time to an orientation phase. We simply revisited this by posing the following questions:

- What is evaluation ?
- Why do we evaluate ?
- How do we evaluate ?

After briefly discussing the responses to these questions, we extended the scope of the study to include:

- How can we give you feedback about the progress of your learning ?

We encouraged the children to brainstorm a list of possible forms of giving feedback. Their final list included methods from their own range of experiences, experiences of older siblings, television and movies, and included such things as marks, grades, points, stars, stamps, written/oral comments.

Setting the study field

Once the children had made a commitment to be involved we collaboratively set about deciding exactly what the peer evaluation panel would assess. Our current unit of study had been entitled 'Why Explore?' and had examined the explorations of the Old World explorers — including Marco Polo,

Da Gama, Columbus, Diaz, Magellan and Henry the Navigator. We had already completed a study of Marco Polo during which we modelled:

- the processes involved in gathering, organising and presenting information
- the processes involved in report writing

We summarised these processes and collaboratively constructed class charts for future reference. We decided to build on this experience. Therefore the field of study became 'Explorers'.

Negotiating the task

Vicki and I gave our students this broad set of parameters:

> From the list below choose an explorer you would like to learn more about. Focus on the following:
> - Who was _____ ?
> - When did he explore ?
> - Why did he explore ?
> - Where did he explore ?
> - Why do you think his exploration/s were important ?
>
> Add any other information you feel is important and organise it as you think best. You may also choose a study partner, have one chosen for you or work independently. The explorers included in the study are Da Gama, Columbus, Diaz, Magellan and Henry the Navigator.

We set these parameters in order to allow us to observe and assess two things:

- what the children had taken from our Marco Polo demonstration in terms of process and content
- the degree to which the children could transfer this learning from one context to another

We intended to use this information to make future decisions at both the macro (whole class) and the micro (individual/group) levels.

We believed that we'd left sufficient scope for them to shape and/or extend the project in ways that suited the data they gathered and the issues that would inevitably arise. Although we provided the option of working individually, we subtly encouraged them to work with a partner. We did this because we wanted them to experience at first hand the benefits of collaborative learning.

Negotiating the evaluation criteria

After clarifying the field of the study we then needed to define the evaluation criteria. Vicki and I spent some time explaining what we believed about the criteria of evaluation and encouraged a free ranging discussion and critique of our beliefs. The beliefs we made explicit included:

- Just as it is important to make the purpose of a learning experience explicit for learners it is important that the evaluation criteria be made explicit for them too.
- This should be done before beginning the learning task.
- We should assess to find out what the learner can do and what they need to learn more about.
- Evaluators should not set out to trick learners.

In the discussion that followed this sharing of our beliefs, the class reached the conclusion that if evaluators didn't make the evaluation criteria explicit before the setting the task they would run the risk of collecting information that was not indicative of learners' real situations. They could therefore make inappropriate judgements and thus render the assessment data invalid.

We then initiated a series of discussions to develop the evaluation criteria for the Explorer project. These discussions focused on the importance of process versus product. While no one disregarded the value of the product, it was generally felt that 'most of the hard work' took place before the publication phase even began! The 'hard work' included deciding who to study, locating and reading relevant support material, making useful research notes, organising the notes into workable units, expanding the notes into sentence form, reworking, conferencing and editing the text ready for publication. The class group therefore decided to evaluate the process by closely examining the learner's working notes and draft. They believed this would give valuable evidence of the learner's understandings of the process and his/her skills.

They also agreed that product should also to be assessed in terms of criteria relating mainly to the use of conventions and illustrations. They argued that if work was 'going public' then it should met the conventions of spelling, punctuation and handwriting. They also decided that illustrations should support the text and that a map outlining the explorer's voyages was mandatory. Finally they decided that a bibliography of the support material consulted should be included.

Determining evaluation feedback

Once the class group reached agreement, this list of criteria was displayed in the room for reference purposes. The next task was to decide the form the feedback would take — should marks, stars, grades be used? The children discussed this and eventually it was decided to give feedback in the form of marks. Now the real work began!

- How many marks could to be given in total?
- How would the marks be allotted among the criteria?
- How would the learner's marks be decided?

While Vicki and I believe that qualitative assessment offers richer and more meaningful data about a learner's development we did not want to impose our bias upon the class group. It was our intention to allow the children to shape and mould the co-researching study so that they would discover and realise the strengths and weaknesses of a different way of assessing, evaluating and reporting.

How many marks could be given in total?

Suggestions varied from 20, 50, 100 and almost every number in between! Eventually the group decided that it didn't really matter what number was chosen as long it allowed scope to assign appropriate marks for the various criteria. The number 50 was chosen as the highest possible mark.

How would the marks be allotted amongst the criteria?

The criteria were grouped into four main categories — text, conventions, illustrations and presentation. Because we had already established the fact that the creation of the text represented the major learning phase, it was decided to assign marks accordingly.

TEXT
- relevancy of the information   /5
- information written in own language style   /5
- notes and draft   /10
Total   /20

The area of conventions was discussed next. The panel would be assessing both spelling and punctuation.

CONVENTIONS
- punctuation   /5
- spelling   /5
Total   /10

The use of illustrations and maps was the next category to be assigned marks. Three criteria were identified here.

ILLUSTRATIONS
- supporting the text   /4
- interesting and relevant   /3
- brightly and neatly presented   /3
Total   /10

The final category was presentation, and again we identified three criteria.

PRESENTATION
- handwriting   /5
- headings and borders   /3
- bibliography   /2

Total   /10

How would the learner's marks be decided?

This of course was an area where the children had little to no experience. We needed to demonstrate this process not only for the children who would form the peer evaluation panel but also for class as a whole, so that everyone was in full possession of the same information, thus avoiding potential doubt or confusion as well as developing and maintaining a shared trust.

After another class discussion it was decided that the peer evaluators would work in pairs. This decision made the children more comfortable because they would have a partner to consult and discuss with and to help in the decision making process: 'I think Connor's handwriting is worth a 4. What do you think?' Vicki and I supported this decision as we believe that partner interaction provides greater opportunities for the development of problem solving and language skills.

After setting up a role play situation demonstrating an evaluation situation we asked the children to identify the procedures we employed. This is what they came up with:
- make sure that study notes, draft and product are present
- write the owner's name and class at the top of the evaluation response sheet
- skim read the study notes, draft and product
- consult a dictionary or reference material to confirm the use of conventions
- discuss the use of illustrations, maps, headings, etc.
- refer to study notes, draft and product to decide upon a mark for each of the criteria
- complete the response sheet by placing a mark in the appropriate space
- tally the marks and complete the general comments section
- file the response sheet in the evaluation folder

We also carefully modelled the need to discuss different points of view. This involved showing how evaluators supported their value judgements by referring to the data they had, including the study notes, the draft, and the product. We also modelled how they reached consensus on the mark to be given by discussion. Through these demonstrations we hoped to impress on the students that marks should not be arbitrary figures plucked from the air or based on the relationship between the owner of the work and the evaluator, but should be a reflection of the learner's 'success' in meeting the negotiated criteria.

Setting a submission date

At the conclusion of this session we recapped the ground already covered to clarify any confusion or misunderstandings. We then proceeded to negotiate a submission date that allowed adequate time for the Explorer project to be completed. We continued to review this date to accommodate unexpected timetable changes, school events such as visiting performers and the availability of support and reference material. At least one hour per day was fully devoted to the study task and daily sharing meetings were conducted to allow progress, problems and findings to be shared. This was an extremely valuable time for the children, enabling them to learn of the problems encountered by other study pairs and the solutions employed to overcome these hurdles. It also offered the opportunity to share and celebrate success in terms of process and content. The session allowed us to collect valuable data recorded in anecdotal form, monitor the progress of the study task and to constantly revisit the evaluation criteria. Once the negotiated date arrived, each child was required to submit his/her study notes, draft and finished product.

The peer evaluation panel

As the submission date drew near it was time to consider the formulation of the peer evaluation panel. Several questions were posed for class discussion:
- What qualities should a peer evaluator display?
- How many members should make up the panel?
- Whom should they be responsible to?

What qualities should a peer evaluator display?

The following list was brainstormed and agreed on:
- a clear understanding of the evaluation criteria
- the ability to work as part of a team
- the ability to remain on task — with/without supervision
- the ability to discuss a point of view and reach agreement
- a real interest in evaluation and learning
- an understanding that there would be a lot of work to do — some in personal free time
- the ability to be impartial — fair to everyone
- to keep information concerning the outcome of individual's evaluations confidential until instructed to do otherwise

Once this list was collated we asked anyone who felt they possessed the above qualities to prepare a brief statement or speech outlining their suitability for panel representation to be presented the following day. Approximately 12 children volunteered to be part of this group and participated in the forum. Vicki and I believed it was essential to adopt this process to ensure all children were aware of the expectations panel membership would bring and ensure a real commitment to the task.

How many members should make up the panel?

The size of the panel would be an important factor in determining its effectiveness. Group dynamics can be severely affected by the number of participants endeavoring to discuss issues and reach agreement. For this reason the class group decided that the panel should be composed of five students — four of whom would work in pairs and a fifth who would act as a co-ordinator. The co-ordinator's role was identified as follows:
• to ensure fairness and diplomacy at all times
• to help in decision-making when consensus appears difficult to reach
• to assume an evaluation role when an evaluator's own work is under consideration
• to dispense and collect the work to be evaluated by the pairs
• to act as 'gopher' and liaise with the teachers
• to ensure all documentation — including evaluation response sheets — is collated

To whom should the panel be responsible?

It was decided that the peer evaluation panel would be directly responsible to the teachers while at the same time providing regular inputs to the class as a whole. These inputs would be to report upon the progress made — 'Today we evaluated four more research assignments leaving another sixteen to complete' — and the general trends noted — 'We have noticed that apostrophes are sometimes used incorrectly' or 'Most people have used maps very well to explain the explorer's journey.'

The peer evaluation panel at work

After listening to the statements made by the prospective peer evaluators, five children were selected by a secret show of hands. Vicki and I were content to give this choice over to the class as we trusted their ability to make a selection based upon the negotiated qualities deemed necessary rather than personal friendships and popular relationships. Had we not been confident of this we may have selected the peer evaluators ourselves. However, we would still have encouraged the interested participants to make their speeches.

The evaluation panel began their task with enthusiasm and excitement. By the end of the first week they began to realise just how much work was actually involved and just how much time it was going to take to complete the evaluation of each piece of work. We had allowed at least an hour per day during the first week but increased that to two hours thereafter. This time could be used flexibly by the panel to help eliminate loss of concentration and accommodate individual differences in attention span. The panel also elected to use some of their free time, working through recess and lunch breaks to ensure the task would be completed in a reasonable amount of time.

Comments like 'We didn't think it would take this long to evaluate each person's work!' and 'We didn't know teachers have to use so much of their own time!' were heard and shared among the whole class. As the task proceeded past the second week a member of the panel expressed a desire to resign due to the pressure of other commitments. This person was also a member of an interschool sporting team and wished to devote more time to training. The peer evaluation panel met, discussed the request and agreed that the member should be allowed to resign and that the co-ordinator should assume the vacated position. They chose not to replace the member from the remainder of the class group as they felt that even though everyone had been exposed to the same preparation, they had developed as a team and believed that the introduction of a new member would necessitate changes to their established routines and consequently slow down their progress.

Vicki and I continued to provide support as required. At times this would take the form of resource persons when the panel was not sure about the use of a particular convention or grammatical structure. Occasionally panel members experienced difficulty when seeking to confirm a particular aspect of the content area or found they could not reach agreement on a mark. We then assumed the role originally fulfilled by the panel co-ordinator. For the most part we were reflective listeners who gathered valuable information to be shared and further explored at a debriefing session, or we were significant others who encouraged and supported as they worked through the task.

Responding to the learner — providing feedback

Because the groups had agreed that the real purpose of evaluation is to provide meaningful feedback to the learner, they next examined the issue of giving feedback that responded to both the learner and the learner's product. Again Vicki and I used a role play to do this. We role played the interaction between a hypothetical evaluator (Coral) and a hypothetical student whose work she had evaluated (Victoria). The demonstration focused on explaining a response sheet with comments, justifying the marks given and providing positive feedback and constructive suggestions. At the end of the role play the children considered some focal questions and discussed them. Here are some examples of this discussion:

How do you think Victoria felt about Coral's responses to her questions?

'I think Victoria felt happy about the answers to her questions because Coral explained the answers really clearly.'

'I think she felt very happy about her work because she got good marks. Coral said nice things to her about her work. She found out what was good about her work.'

How do you think Victoria felt about her work?

'Victoria felt confident enough to say what she felt about her work.'

'Victoria thought her work was good, set out well, her border was nice, her writing neat and her pictures were good.'

What did Coral do to help Victoria?

'Coral told Victoria what to do on her next research study so she can learn. She was nice to Victoria and didn't say any negative things.'

'Coral told Victoria what she could do for her next assignment — check over her work to make sure about everything before she hands her work in.'

Through this role play the evaluation panel became aware of their responsibility to provide appropriate feedback and the rest of the class developed an expectation of the feedback encounter.

The evaluation-feedback encounter

Again the evaluation panel reformed their original pairings and began the feedback process. After seeking approval from all, Vicki and I installed a cassette recorder at each of the two sites and also sat in on the discussion as observers, only entering the dialogue when invited to do so. We were amazed and delighted with the manner in which the children conducted themselves. The evaluators provided detailed feedback in an honest and supportive manner. They were aware their peers had handed them much more than a research study — they had in fact 'laid themselves on the line' and entrusted their confidence and self-esteem to the panel. Some feedback taken from the transcripts included:

'We could see how much work you did in your draft. You did a lot of editing. We gave you 9/10. What do you think about that?'

'We didn't find any spelling mistakes in your published text. We gave you 5/5.'

'We thought your published work would look better if your handwriting went the same way. Some goes up and down and some goes backwards. We gave you 2/5 because you used ruled lines to write on.'

'We gave you 3/5 for punctuation because sometimes you forgot to use a capital letter at the beginning of a sentence or for the name of a country.'

'Your illustrations were bright and neat so we gave you 2/3. If your coloring-in had gone all the one way you would have got a 3/3.'

General written comments at the end of the response sheet were as follows:

'Keep up the good work!'

'We enjoyed reading your work.'

'Suzi your work was really good. Keep it up!'

During the course of the feedback session, students would ask why they received a particular mark or what they could do to improve their work. Almost every child thanked both evaluators for the time and effort they had spent on their work. They were required to collect their work and record relevant thoughts and ideas in their personal learning journals. Because Vicki and I believe evaluation is not an end in itself we reinforced the notion that this information was to be referred to in future learning situations. Some children drew on this feedback to help formulate personal learning goals, as outlined earlier in this chapter.

Results of the peer evaluation project

From the reflection and discussion that followed the peer feedback sessions Vicki and I identified certain learning outcomes for the following participants:

The class group

Learners were able to verbalise a greater understanding of the nature of evaluation and its role within the learning process:

'The panel told me what I did good and how I can improve my work. I need to read more information next time. I didn't have enough details.'

'I learnt a lot about Vasco Da Gama because I had lots of information to read and I made good notes. My study partner helped me too.'

'The panel told me to check my spelling before I hand my work in. I made mistakes in the little words.'

'I think this was a good thing to do because we learnt about evaluation criteria. We knew what the panel was looking for when they talked about our work.'

'I think this was a good idea because the panel told me how to make my work look better. I need to make my writing go one way.'

'My study partner helped me understand some hard words in the information. We talked about it and then I made my work better.'

'The panel had a hard job to do. It took a lot of time to read all the assignments and decide a mark for everyone.'

The peer evaluation panel

Vicki and I asked the members of the peer evaluation panel to record their thoughts and feelings in their learning journals. Following are Lilly's thoughts relating to her experience:

Being a panel member is fun but you have a hard job to do because you have to be sure of what mark you give. You have to co-operate with each panel member, listen to their ideas and support them in any way you can. We all have to keep it confidential and not have any arguments about it. The hard thing about it is marking the assignment that doesn't have drafts, references and other things that are supposed to be included. Also being on the panel is a hard responsibility because you have to discuss a lot of things such as are the drafts suitable for year six standard. When you come to the marking part you have to look at things like: is it presented neatly, are the drafts included, is there a reference and is it presented properly. When giving a mark you need to talk to the others and share opinions to give a fair mark. You also have to be very confidential and you have to discuss it in an adult manner, that's part of being a member of the panel.

In her journal entry Suzi discussed the feelings she experienced while listening to her work being assessed by two other panel members. She was participating in the evaluation of another piece at the time, but found it difficult to concentrate fully upon her own task. She described her feelings as uncomfortable, anxious and a little embarrassed at what the comments might be. Similar experiences helped to make all panel members more sensitive to the feelings of those they evaluated.

What we'd do differently if we did it again

Vicki and I have some ideas about the development of the peer evaluation component of the study. We would like to develop this concept further, perhaps through a comparative study which addressed the question: 'What kind of information (mark, grade, comment sheet) provides the learner with the most valuable form of feedback?'

If we did such a study we would modify what we did this time so that learners could clearly identify the value of each of these methods of feedback. We would probably present the learners with only a numerical mark and later follow this with a response sheet and ask them which form of feedback gave them 'richer' or more usable information about what they had done well or what they could improve upon. In other words, we would be asking them to compare the quantitative and qualitative data in terms of value to them and their parents.

CONCLUSION

Vicki and I were constantly amazed and excited by the connections and understandings the children shared with us. Neither of us was fully aware of the direction or shape the project would take. We merely provided the framework and the environment and the children took over the study and moulded and shaped it themselves. The level of sophistication at which the learners operated constantly inspired us. It is a powerful example of what children are capable of achieving if only we are willing to 'let go' and support them as they come to terms with learning itself. We share the utmost admiration for the learners who shared this study with us.

8

Interpreting data

How do we make sense of what we collect?

by Brian Cambourne, Jan Turbill & Dianne Dal Santo

*Gathering data is only one part of the
assessment and evaluation process; unless we
can interpret the data we collect it is not of
much use in informing us of student
learning. Interpretation refers to the creation
of meaning from data In this chapter,
Brian Cambourne, Jan Turbill &
Dianne Dal Santo help us to unpack the
processes that are involved in the process of
interpretation. This process is slowed down
and opened up in order to bring to our
conscious awareness what we seem to be able
to do intuitively and automatically. This has
been done because Brian, Jan and Dianne
believe that when you can make these
processes explicit you have a better chance
of understanding and therefore using
them effectively.*

Stage 4 on the conceptual map of responsive evaluation (p. 19) is labelled 'Interpreting data'. We deliberately chose the term 'data', rather than 'information' to make this point:

• Data are different from information.

Data are facts. You can collect and produce large amounts of data in the form of facts and figures, but this is not information. Information is the meaning that human minds assign to these facts. Information is created by individual minds drawing on individual experience, separating the trivial from the relevant, and making value judgements. Information leads to understanding and knowledge.

It is only when facts (data) are processed by the human mind that information becomes possible. This process of turning data into information is what we mean by 'interpretation'.

We found that before we could move on to Stage 5 ('Reporting to audiences') we had first to know how we turned our data into information.

We couldn't find any advice in the literature about this process. Some writers acknowledged it was important but few gave us any clues on how it is done, leading us to conclude that one of the things that has been missing from recent attempts to develop programs of assessment and evaluation has been any theoretical base that will inform the processes of interpretation. In this chapter we intend to discuss what we found.

THE NATURE OF INTERPRETATION

At one level there is nothing very esoteric or abstract about the process of interpretation. It is part of the meaning-making behavior that we do quite naturally. Every day we are in a constant state of data gathering. Every day we take in huge amounts of data and are continually interpreting it. Every day we interpret this data (turn it in to information) in order to make a range of decisions, many of which are evaluative in nature in that they involve the weighing-up of different kinds of evidence from a range of contexts.

Let's look at an everyday example. Imagine a young couple who decide to sell their old car and buy a new one. Before deciding on which car to buy they gather a great deal of data — they talk to people, they visit car dealers, they read brochures, they look at different cars parked at the supermarket, and may also read the car section in newspapers. Finally they need to make some judgements about all these data. So with some very important criteria in their heads they start to turn it into information. They start sorting the data into categories which grow out of their needs:

- they only have a certain amount of money
- they will only drive in the suburbs and city
- they want something that will last ten or more years
- they intend to start a family soon
- they both want to be able to drive it so it needs to be an easy car to drive — automatic if possible

They then sit down and list the categories — safety features, ease of getting things in and out of back seat and boot, manoeuvrability in the city streets, and price. Under each of these four headings they list the data they have collected for each of the cars they have seen. They organise these facts, sorting and bundling them together, turning them into information that helps them clearly see the pros and cons of each car. This is 'interpretation'. It turns data into information. If done well it leads them to feel confident that they are making the right decision.

Teachers who want to evaluate their students' learning are in a similar position. They collect large amounts of data about their learners (that is, they assess) and then they have to turn these data into information (that is, interpret it), before they can make any judgement about it (that is, before they can evaluate it).

What is interesting is that teachers are doing this all day. They can't help it. Typically they're doing it unconsciously, 'on the run', as they move through the course of a teaching day. Every decision they make as they interact with their students or plan what they are going to do in the next few seconds or minutes is based on an interpretation of the data coming at them, pushed through a cognitive framework of what they think their students need to learn or do at that particular time. Like most other subconscious and automatic processes (such as talking or reading) we tend to take it for granted, never thinking too much about how or why it works the way it does. One of our informants described it as 'unverbalisable know-how', others called it 'intuition. Essentially it seemed to involve some kind 'tacit' (subconscious) knowledge.

HOW TEACHERS INTERPRET DATA: WHAT WE FOUND OUT

How do teachers manage to make sense of all the information they collect? How do they interpret?

This was one of the many questions we addressed in the project. We asked a number of our co-researchers to be informants. We spent many hours trying to help them turn this tacit knowledge into 'propositional' (explicit) knowledge. When we in turn interpreted the data they gave us, we found that while there some differences in how they went about interpreting, these were far outweighed by the commonalities they shared. Here is a summary of the main things we found:

What these teachers did

- Teachers were continually collecting data as they observed, listened to, talked with, questioned, interviewed, collected products, etc. in the day-to-day ebb and flow of classroom life.
- Teachers were continually turning this data into information and interpreting it.
- For most of the time they interpreted and made decisions based on these interpretations 'on the run'. They kept this information in their heads.
- Teachers usually formalised and made explicit these 'in the head interpretations' (wrote them down) for two reasons:
  - when they were asked by someone else to be accountable for what they teach
  - when they needed to do some long term planning

How they did it

- They reduced the complexity of the data they had collected by sorting it into a small number of categories.
- They then gave each of these categories a descriptive label.
- The categories they chose grew out of what they believed about the nature of effective literacy.
- Typically they created between three and five categories which become a kind of framework for interpretation. (We decided to call this framework an 'interpretive frame'.)

We were encouraged by the discovery that another group of Canadian researchers, working in a similar way, had come to similar conclusions. They found that interpretation involved at least the following four processes (Anthony et al. 1991, p.106):

1 Gather discrete information
2 Cluster findings into related sets or patterns
3 Describe the general character of these sets or patterns
4 Review the portfolio for corroborating evidence

We felt a great deal of resonance with items 2 and 3 in their list.

AN EXAMPLE OF THE PROCESS OF INTERPRETATION IN ACTION

How does this process look in practice?

In what follows we explore the processes involved in interpretation by focusing on the work of one of our co-researchers (Dianne Dal Santo). The processes she identified are representative of what the rest of our co-researchers also identified as we worked on this project.

At the time that this research was done Dianne was teaching a Year 6 class in a school classified as eligible for support from the Disadvantaged Schools Program (DSP) because of its multicultural composition: just over 400 pupils, in which the overwhelming majority were from non-English speaking backgrounds, coming from 28 different language groups.

We began by asking Dianne to explain the process she'd gone through to design and implement her version of responsive evaluation. She told us that she:

- became consciously aware of her values, beliefs, philosophy, that related to literacy and why she thought she was teaching it;
- developed a workable set of data collecting (assessment) procedures;
- developed a set of categories for organising data (an interpretive frame);
- sorted data into these categories;
- asked 'What does the way that my data are distributed in these categories mean?' (interpretation)

The belief system/philosophy

Dianne's summarised her philosophy of literacy teaching:

At the core of my philosophy is a strong belief that I should be setting up conditions that would produce life-long readers and writers. I believe this is important because I also believe that engaging in sustained reading and writing is the best way possible of getting control of language, and language in turn is the medium of thinking, learning, knowing, understanding and problem solving. It is this control of language that I consider to capture the essence of 'literacy'. I also believe that literacy is more than knowledge of facts which can be automatically called into play, like letter sound correspondences, the spellings of words, or the conventions of grammar and punctuation. There is a meta-cognitive level to this kind of knowledge. Learners who are consciously aware of how this knowledge can be used become better readers writers, spellers, etc. Effective reading, writing, spelling, talking, listening are based on a range of processes and strategies that must be brought under control before they can be brought into play. These strategies are made up of clusters of single skills which are best brought under control if they are taught from whole to part. The most effective way to pull these skills together into clusters that can operate as strategies is in the context of other single skills they support and are in turn supported by. Finally I also believe that literacy is a kind of 'cultural capital' that empowers those who have acquired it by providing a resource that puts access to power and social equity within their reach.

The data collecting procedures

Dianne collected data on her students using a similar range of procedures to those described in Chapters 3, 5 and 6. She observed, interviewed, collected samples of children's work. She turned her observations into field notes which she called anecdotal records. She also asked her students to keep records that could be used as data. Accordingly they kept reading logs and learning logs which she regularly sampled. She used the products of such learning activities as retellings, proofreading, weekly contracts, as data.

The interpretive frame

Dianne began to explain this point by saying:

Learners' needs can be very complex. There is simply too much to take into account without first developing some way of organising the data that is continually being gathered. I worked out that I needed to develop a set of categories that would help me control all the data I was collecting if I wanted to make evaluative decisions about what I should do or plan to do next.

Dianne based her interpretive frame on the beliefs she'd made explicit at Stage 1 of the map. Here are the categories she developed. We have placed them in table format to show how they link to her beliefs and overall philosophy.

Categories that make up interpretive frame	Link to beliefs
Attitude (towards literacy)	I should be setting up conditions that would produce life-long readers and writers because engaging in sustained reading and writing is the best way possible of getting control of language, and language in turn is the medium of thinking, learning, knowing, understanding and problem solving.
Knowledge of literacy processes	I also believe that literacy is more than knowledge of facts which can be automatically called into play, like letter-sound correspondences, the spelling of words, or the conventions of grammar and punctuation. There is a meta-cognitive level to this kind of knowledge. Learners who are consciously aware of how this knowledge can be used become better readers, writers and spellers.
Single literacy skills under control	Literacy processes are made up of clusters of single skills which are best brought under control if they are taught from whole to part.
Literacy strategies (clusters of skills) under control	[Literacy] strategies are made up of clusters of single skills which are best brought under control if they are taught from whole to part. The most effective way to pull these skills together into clusters that can operate as strategies is in the context of other single skills they support and are supported by.

Our next question was:
• How are these interpretive frames used?
We found out that it is the same as what a good field anthropologist or good ethnographer does, namely read through all the information which has been collected and place it in the appropriate category.
Our next question was:
• How does this actually look in practice?
Let's revisit Dianne's interpretive frame. On reading through her field notes on one of her students her teacher's eye was drawn to comments such as:

- *Slave [pronounced Slarvay] was quick to select a book from the class collection and settled quickly to read during SSR. He looked at the cover of the book, flicked through it, stopped and read small sections then decided to read.*

- *During SSR time Slave was on task.*

- *Slave was willing to contribute ideas in the discussion I led on how seas and oceans were formed.*

She believed that these three comments were markers of some of the attitudes which Slave held about literacy. So she intuitively placed them in the Attitude row in her mental interpretive frame. It would have looked something like this.

Categories which make up interpretive frame	Data which 'fit' the category
Attitude (towards literacy)	Feb 9: Slave was quick to select a book from the class collection and settled quickly to read during SSR. He looked at the cover of the book, flicked through it stopped and read small sections and then decided to read. Feb 12: During SSR time Slave was on task. Feb 13: Slave was willing to contribute to the discussion I lead on how seas and oceans were formed.

On another occasion when looking through Slave's learning log she found a number of his entries that reflected both his attitude and his growth in knowledge of literacy processes.

29/3/90:

Today I learnt it's a good idea for you to read a story and get an idea from it and change the characters, the place that it's in and rearrange the story line. You can also write about something that has happened to you in real life.

29/5/90:

I sometimes enjoy reading and sometimes I don't, it depends because sometimes all the books I read seem very boring to me but sometimes when I'm in the mood I'll read the most boring book in the world and still enjoy it. Also if I find a book that I really like I'll read it very fast. I mostly choose a book by its cover. But sometimes by its title or sometimes I choose it if a friend has read it and they say it's good.

As before, Dianne intuitively placed this information in the appropriate category. Her internal unconscious interpretive frame would have now looked like this.

Categories which make up interpretive frame	Data which 'fit' the category
Attitude (towards literacy)	Feb 9: Slave was quick to select a book from the class collection and settled quickly to read during SSR. He looked at the cover of the book, flicked through it stopped and read small sections and then decided to read. Feb 12: During SSR time Slave was on task. Feb 13: Slave was willing to contribute to the discussion I lead on how seas and oceans were formed. 29/3/90: Today I learnt it's a good idea for you to read a story and get an idea from it and change the characters, the place that it's in and rearrange the story line. You can also write about something that has happened to you in real life.
Knowledge of literacy processes	2/5/90: I sometimes enjoy reading and sometimes I don't, it depends because sometimes all the books I read seem very boring to me but sometimes when I'm in the mood I'll read the most boring book in the world and still enjoy it. Also if I find a book that I really like I'll read it very fast. I mostly choose a book by its cover. But sometimes by its title or sometimes I choose it if a friend has read it and they say it's good.

Dianne repeats this process as she goes through the portfolio of data she's collected about Slave. Try to imagine each of the categories in her interpretive frame being filled with data drawn from the records of her observations (her anecdotal records), the student learning logs, the products she'd decided to collect (including the results of some teaching/learning activities like proofreading and retelling) her recordings of the interactions and conversations she'd had with her students. When she has done this she has turned data into information.

Turning data into information

Because these categories are derived from her belief system they are by definition 'meaningful'. The way she distributes her data across these categories begins to imbue them with meaning. They stop being 'data' and begin to turn into 'information'. The final thing that Dianne does is ask:

• What does the way that my data are distributed in these categories mean?

To begin to answer this question she has to pull two sources of information together:

(i) the information in the categories she created

(ii) the deep pool of tacit knowledge of things she'd witnessed and not recorded, plus her beliefs and values about what was important about literacy

The interaction of these two sources of information it what enables her to begin making value judgements about each students' learning.

CONCLUSION

It needs to be restated that Dianne doesn't take the time to laboriously rearrange all the information she has collected and then laboriously fill out separate tables for each organiser and then laboriously interpret the result as it she were doing some kind of intricate research project. Like most teachers she can dip into her huge data pool of information, crosscheck, come to conclusions and make decisions. Her previous attempts to make her beliefs, values, philosophy explicit has given her the confidence to do all this mentally at great speed. She can then justify and/or crosscheck the validity of any decisions she makes from the data she has collected.

9
Creating a community of learners for change

by Roy Williams

Chapters 4, 5, 6, 7 and 8 focused on how individual teachers took the theoretical principles behind responsive evaluation and turned them into classroom practice. While it might be said that individual classrooms are mini-cultures in their own right, schools are also cultures in their own right. They are more than the sum of the individual classes that comprise them. They develop as a consequence of all the roles and pressures that outside agencies and individuals bring to the school setting, from the students, teachers and parents to state mandated syllabuses and curricula and state officials and administrators.

This is the level at which school principals must work, especially if they want to bring about changes in the culture that they believe will impact positively on student learning.

How can principals change the culture of schools, especially in something as sensitive as introducing a new and different approach to the assessment and evaluation of student learning? In this chapter, Roy Williams tells the story of how he went about changing the culture of his school so that responsive evaluation could work to promote optimal learning for all.

BACKGROUND

Farmborough Road School is like most other schools in the Wollongong area of New South Wales. There are approximately 600 students from a range of socio-economic and ethnic backgrounds, 21 teachers, five other executive staff and myself, the principal. Like many other schools we have been struggling with the issues of assessment and evaluation. What follows is the story of our journey (over some rather rough terrain at times) towards the development of an evaluation policy which results in optimal learning for all.

At the beginning of the journey we needed to define for ourselves and the community we served the terms 'assessment' and 'evaluation'. We decided that generally 'assessment' meant the gathering of information for the purposes of making judgements, whereas 'evaluation' was the process of making judgements on what had been gathered. As one presupposes the other we decided that we would use the term 'evaluation' to mean both processes rather than keep using the two terms. This decision was the first of many that began the process of developing a shared meaning through shared language amongst the teachers, the parents and the students.

If we were to operate as a 'community of learners' in the sense that Barth (1991) in his insightful book on school change, *Improving Schools from Within* advocates, we had to develop a learning culture which included teachers, parents and students. The analogy of Stromberg (1982, p.1) which Barth cites reflected clearly the kind of culture I wanted to create in my school.

And one day, lying alone on the lawn on my back, hearing only the moan and groan of some far off train on a distant track, I saw above me, 2000 feet or more, something which to this day, I must say, I've never seen anything like before. The head goose, the leader of the 'V', suddenly swerved out, leaving a vacancy that promptly was filled by the bird behind. The leader then flew alongside, the formation growing wide, and took his place at the back of the line — and they never missed a beat! ... I found out that those geese can fly from way up north to way down south, and back again. But they cannot do it alone, you see. It's something they must do as a community. Oh, I know, it's a popular notion, and people swell with pride and emotion to think of themselves on the eagle side — strong, self-confident, solitary. Not bad traits. But we are what we are — that's something we can't choose. And though many of us would like to be seen as the eagle, I think God made us more like the Goose.'

A wonderful description of the culture that is collegial and collaborative; it's what we hoped to develop so that change would be enjoyable, challenging, rewarding and worthwhile!

In *Frameworks: The Assessment and Evaluation Module* (1994), Cambourne, Turbill, Butler and Langton argue that the four criteria of effective evaluation are:

- assessment and evaluation must result in optimal learning for all involved;
- assessment and evaluation must inform, support and justify teacher decision-making;

- assessment and evaluation practices must reflect the theories of language, learning and literacy which guide our teaching;
- the findings which result from our assessment and evaluation practices must be accurate, valid, reliable, and perceived to be rigorous by all who use them.

In this chapter I want to describe how we, the staff at Farmborough Road Elementary School, involved all elements of an educational community in the task of developing an evaluation policy that meets these four criteria. As school leader I played a range of roles varying from 'leading from the rear' to 'carrying the flag' and 'deflecting the flak'. Decisions on when and how to move in and out of these various roles presented a challenge requiring at times a very delicate balancing act. The outcomes were worth it!

OUR EVALUATION MODEL

It was important that we first decided on a model of evaluation so that we all had a shared understanding of what was driving our policy. As a group we decided that we wanted:

- parents to share and gain knowledge along with us in learning about their children in the learning process: to share experiences and outcomes with their children and discuss these freely with the teacher, student and other school personnel;
- students to learn about themselves and their place in the learning process: to share with their parents and constantly negotiate with their teachers with regard to their curriculum and evaluation;
- teachers to facilitate the learning process and negotiate with their students, share and celebrate successes with the parents which would lead to satisfying, relevant and constructive individual evaluation for the student.

We recognised that:

- teachers performed many types of evaluation daily, but like most schools we lacked a school-wide plan for collection and use of information;
- school staff needed to define and put into operation common goals for evaluation;
- curriculum goals, instructional strategies, and evaluation activities needed to be based the same learning theory and occur simultaneously, otherwise there would be a massive waste of time and effort leading to gross inefficiency and ineffectiveness in the learning process.

The model we developed to guide and frame our policy is shown in Figure 9.1.

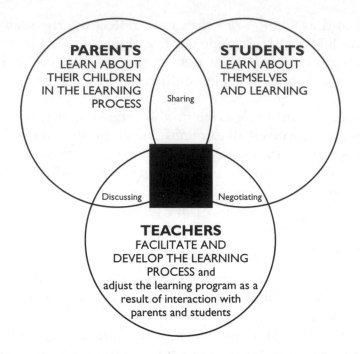

Figure 9. 1 Farmborough Road School evaluation model

It can be clearly seen from the model that we saw teachers, parents and students as key people in the evaluation process. But there were other people to whom we needed to report student progress, such as the central office administrators. We therefore needed to consider the purposes for reporting student progress and the range of audiences to whom we were expected to report the information. We saw the need to communicate to the array of stakeholders in the educative process what and how students had learned in a period of time. Teachers, parents and students were the first order stakeholders, whilst central office administration, policy makers, politicians, employers, and the media were viewed as the second order stakeholders.

None of what occurred over the next two and a half years could have been done without the establishment of a learning culture in which change was an accepted way of living, and the support of many capable, committed and dedicated classroom teachers working together towards a common goal based on developed and developing beliefs, knowledge, understanding, support, faith and trust. Although we began as a few committed people, our community of learners grew as others began to develop a sense of commitment and ownership through the development of a shared meaning and language of what our overall goals were. We were all in there, after all, for the betterment of learning outcomes for 'our kids'.

When asked to describe the type of culture that they would like to see developed at our school, two valued colleagues from our school wrote:

The culture of the school involves the values, attitudes, assumptions and beliefs of those involved in its organisation. It is the perception of members of the organisation about nature of that organisation, including such aspects as decision making and problem solving. The norms of behavior of the school have been accepted by members of the organisation and reflect their shared beliefs. The assumptions which, like the norms, are tacit and unwritten, deal with what organisation members see as being right or wrong and are not often discussed, yet are still accepted and exert a strong influence on behavior.

... Decision making is the responsibility of the stakeholders. The more effect the decision has on the community, staff or students the greater the input they should have. The more ownership felt by those involved, the more effective the change will be. The analysis of needs perceived by staff, students and community must be used as the basis for a plan, where priorities are given to areas seen to be most needy. In this way, vision will be shared and the change will be seen as purposeful and worthwhile. Where staff and community work co-operatively together in a relationship of trust and mutual respect, the process of change can be effectively implemented.

(Linda, Year 4 teacher)

I believe that in establishing a climate and culture within a school, many factors must be considered and a vision held which encompasses all elements necessary for organisational renewal. Such issues as leadership style, management of conflict and managing the change process need to be considered and built into the vision. This vision needs to be a shared vision, made explicit and supported by structures which need to be established within the school. There needs to be developed an awareness of the possible existence of multiple cultures and the distinctive attributes which these may possess, as well as the past histories and experiences of the people involved, as these may exert a powerful influence on belief systems, values and the establishment of trust and collaborative processes.

(Val, Year 2 teacher)

Two very powerful statements displaying the beliefs and commitment of significant co-learners.

What follows are the phases we went through as we developed our evaluation policy. Although it sounds a 'lock-step' and linear process, let me say right now — it was not! There were many times when I thought it would have been easier and less stressful (to me at least) if I could have said — do it this way! But I knew from my past experience and my reading of people like Roland Barth and Michael Fullan that if change was to occur which was deep and lasting then everyone involved had to take part and had to feel a sense of commitment and ultimately ownership of the policy.

PHASE 1: INITIATING THE PROJECT

In initiating any project, I believe, it is necessary to firstly establish a 'platform of success'. This platform is established through the identification of those people in the school who are perceived to have already achieved various successes and are seen to have a vision, and/or are influenced by the visionaries. It is my experience that this ensures that any 'new' initiative carried out by this group of people has the potential for success. This success then ripples across other members of staff. There was a small group of teachers in the school who had begun working in a joint university/school project on evaluation and assessment issues. This group and the project they were involved in became my platform of success. It was important at this point that the rest of the staff knew of our intentions and so we spent a considerable amount of time, both formally and informally, sharing with the staff what was being trialled in their classrooms by those involved in the project. Not only did this process occur with the remaining staff, but at the monthly parent meetings as well. I began letting parents know about this project and the exciting outcomes that were beginning to occur in the classrooms. It was important that all those involved — parents and teachers – knew what we were wanting to achieve in an evaluation policy in the school. Out of this process of sharing and discussing, a shared meaning began to develop, and a sense of commitment to a school evaluation policy evolved.

This small group became the basis for the school committee which was led by a Kindergarten teacher. She was assisted by other volunteer teachers and parents who believed that student evaluation could and should be changed for the better, and who believed that there is more to evaluation than percentages, grades, ticks and position in class. It was this group which began the process of identifying the issues and implications of developing an evaluation policy in our school which would support and enhance student instruction.

An outcome of this process was a calculated and thorough immersion of staff and parents in the philosophies and beliefs which had to be developed in order for changes to be initiated effectively. There had to be innumerable inputs, demonstrations and modelling exercises to alter the views of those stakeholders who still held traditional views on evaluation.

PHASE 2: DELIBERATION PERIOD

Then comes the most difficult and painful phase, that of deliberation. All personnel were encouraged through meetings, workshops and surveys to monitor the progress of the initiative, to share successes and concerns and freely discuss anything relating to our project. It is during this phase that the 'blood is let'. Some of those not involved directly travel into the 'room of denial'. 'Why should I try this? I've been doing what I've been doing for X years. Who needs this? And who can convince me that it will work?' Others move into the 'room of confusion'. 'Perhaps they might have something! My beliefs of X years are being challenged. There might be a better way!'

This is a long and difficult but most necessary phase. This is where discussion and negotiation take place. Working groups are formed. Position papers are prepared and presented. Proposals are put to full staff meetings. Concerns are expressed and acknowledged. Solutions are sought co-operatively and collaboratively. All this takes time and patience!

WARNING! In the change process nothing, in my opinion, should ever go to a vote. Voting is a tool of politics, not democracy. Voting delineates 'winners' and 'losers' and neither really wins. In this type of culture winners are the best and most emotive canvassers and harassers (and often tellers of half truths or even liars). The voters are seldom happy with the decisions and have often changed their minds before clearing the doors of the meeting rooms. Many participants are, unfortunately, partly or ill-informed. If a vote is taken on the same issue the following week the result would probably be quite different. Voting doesn't improve matters. Knowledge, understanding and consideration solve problems. Very few issues are clear and resolvable through a ballot. Issues must be raised without fear and discussed and resolved before progress can be made. 'Voting is the refuge of the wimp.'

The first whole-school meeting

Evaluation had been identified in the school/community needs analysis and was consequently adopted as one of the school's major priorities. To heighten awareness and add impetus to the project the committee organised a whole-school meeting. We sought some funding from the regional office so that we could have a 4.00–9.00pm dinner meeting with staff, parents and community members. We invited key personnel from the local university to present the most up-to-date perspective. During the course of the evening we examined 'our learning theory' and identified the needs and expectations of staff and parents. As a result of this meeting there was much clarification of ideas and elimination of misconceptions of how learning takes place and, in particular, language learning and evaluation.

One significant outcome of this workshop based on our own personal learning experiences was a combined parent/teacher compilation of what constituted our learning theory. This was subsequently printed and distributed and finally featured prominently in the school's evaluation policy. This theory is stated in simple language but represents a very powerful statement of how learning takes place. More significantly, it represents, reflects and pays respect to all those educators (parents and teachers) involved.

Our learning theory
- We begin with
  a need, a desire, a motivation, a problem, a goal, an obligation
- Learning is associated with feelings of:
  fear, apprehension, doubt about capabilities, excitement, confidence
- To help us get started we often:
  seek help (reading, observation, demonstrations, ask someone)
  draw on previous knowledge
  have a visual image of ourselves succeeding
  develop a plan of attack
- We then:
  'have a go', hands on, make mistakes, take risks, display perseverance
- We receive feedback:
  if negative, must be accompanied by support
  if positive, will probably lead to success
- As a result of this feedback we will:
  seek help, accept encouragement, reflect, evaluate
- When our learning has been successful we will:
  celebrate, show off, want to learn more, feel self-satisfied, have a warm inner glow

(Workshop, May, 1991)

Figure 9. 2 Our learning theory

PHASE 3: EXPERIMENTATION AND DEVELOPMENT

We were now off and running. Following that first meeting a booklet was produced summarising staff and parent perceptions of evaluation prior to and at the workshop. This was distributed to staff and parents at subsequent meetings as well as informally. The process now in action was the key to the success of the project. Constant contact, referral, discussion, consultation, revision and amendment now became the feature of the venture.

Staff met frequently and began to produce samples of recording formats, particularly in English and mathematics, from their present and previous experiences as well as from colleagues and other schools. From these samples a booklet was produced by the committee and teachers were encouraged to use this to experiment with a range of new and different evaluation ideas. Likewise, examples of formats for reporting to parents were gathered and reproduced. These were shared with colleagues and discussed with parents at staff and parent meetings over the year. As a consequence, several report formats were developed and submitted to the stakeholders for opinion. A report form was eventually accepted but there was much trepidation about differing interpretations by parents. To solve this foreshadowed problem two lengthy and detailed booklets, a 'Teacher Report Pack' and a 'Parent Report Pack' were produced. The teacher pack looked in detail at the key curriculum areas and contributed to consistency in approach and interpretation. It suggested appropriate language to be used in describing student performance. The parent pack also described in detail the principles of the key curriculum areas, discussed the areas that would receive major concentration, and outlined the type of language that would be used.

This venture occupied much time because of the consultative nature of the approach. The packs were eventually launched at meetings, both evening and daytime, involving parents and teachers. To assist in the understandings of the packs, teachers produced a supporting video in the proposed reporting-to-parents format. The video displayed children involved in the full range of learning activities in and outside their classrooms and conveyed to parents the nature of the learning taking place and the need for parallel procedures to describe this learning. Multiple copies of the video were made and hired to parents for further viewing.

Some examples of what we did at the meetings

By sharing some of the material that was presented to the two hundred parents who attended these two meetings I hope to convey our rationale, theory, intentions and some of the strategies that were to be utilised. At this stage I felt that it was vital that I, as principal, should be 'up front' and seen as an enthusiastic leader and supporter of a unified staff movement to provide a better service to the parents of our students.

1. Establishing credibility with parents

To establish theoretical support and credibility, several quotations from educators and academics from a range of backgrounds were shared and used to support and strengthen our proposals. Included here are a few of them.

As scores become important, students become invisible. (Watson 1989)

The bottom line of my objection is firstly, that 'tests' (in the traditional sense) are not natural, they are not part of the communicative demands of the real world. Secondly, test situations are foreign to my whole language/naturalistic classroom environment. To introduce them would break the trust that I have established with my students based on the belief that we engage in language to further our understandings about the world and ourselves and in this sense language is real and meaningful. As a facilitator and a co-learner I am not out to 'trick', 'catch them out' or 'error hunt' anything my students engage in. What I am interested in is how they are growing in their communicative ability and how my monitoring interaction and analysis can provide feedback that informs their learning processes. (Hancock 1991)

When you take an outcome-oriented approach, you focus on things that are easily quantified. (Brandt 1989)

Let us consider what it is a human-as-instrument can do that the test cannot do. First the human is a responsive instrument. It can respond to all the personal and environmental cues which exist in the assessment context. Secondly it is adaptable. It can collect information about multiple factors at multiple levels, simultaneously. Thirdly, it is 'smart'. Like a 'smart bomb' it can home in on information, change direction, run down leads, follow a trial, and ultimately hit the target. It can clarify, process, explore, summarise, triangulate on the spot and of a host of other things that standardised instruments could never do. In short it can cope with complexities much more effectively and quickly than any testing instrument. (Cambourne 1988)

'The more we focus on raising test scores, the more instruction is distorted, and the less credible are the scores themselves. (Shephard 1989)

In sports, as in reading, one can master component skills and still not play the game very well. (Pearson and Valencia 1987)

These quotations had great impact on parents, who found it difficult to argue against their implications.

2. Evaluation procedures workshop

A useful workshop which we carried out with parents was one we as a staff had experienced during our participation in the staff development program, 'Frameworks'. Parents were asked to complete the grid in Figure 9.3. It asks for the identification of the most useful and appropriate evaluation procedures arranged along the top axis, from those most in context with the task to least-contextual procedures. Without exception, parents identified strategies in the left-hand columns. It was also pointed out that the objectives in the vertical axis were of a very high order and very relevant to the

OBSERVATION GRID								
HOW? **PROCEDURES**	OBSERVATION	LISTENING TO STUDENTS	QUESTIONING CHILDREN	WORK SAMPLES	TEACHER MADE TESTS	CRITERION REFERENCED TESTS	BOOK TESTS	STANDARDISED TESTS
WHAT? **Objectives/Outcomes**	Contextual … Decontextual							
– To express self: to express personal feelings, reactions, values, interests and attitudes								
– To narrate: to tell a fictional story or give an account of real events								
– To inform: to make factual information clear								
– To persuade: to change the opinion of, or influence the action of the audience								
– To describe: to use words that appeal to the senses in order to reveal appearance or to convey image or impression								
– To read for aesthetic or personal response								
– To read for acquisition, interpretation and application of information								
– To read for critical analysis and evaluation								

Figure 9.3: Evaluation grid (Frameworks 1991, Turbill, Butler & Cambourne)

acquisition of worthwhile literacy: 'To describe: to use words that appeal to the senses in order to reveal appearance or to convey image or impression'. This is certainly a more relevant objective than to identify the adverbial clauses in a passage, a skill which some parents in our early meeting had requested should be 'tested'. This activity focused the parents' attention on the fact that the primary purpose of obtaining information is to gain a better understanding of the whole child and to better develop appropriate teaching/learning programs based on abilities, interests and needs.

Parents were as amazed as we had been when we did the workshop, at how much we rely on procedures such as observation, questioning and talking to students as ways of obtaining the most useful information in order to evaluate their progress and their future needs.

Parents were then invited to share and discuss the set of beliefs about evaluation which were again borrowed from 'Frameworks'. These, in the context of the quotations discussed earlier and the grid exercise outlined above, presented a very powerful argument for a qualitative approach to student evaluation.

Our beliefs about evaluation

Evaluation is an ongoing process, occurring before, during and after instruction.

Evaluation includes the process, not just the product.

Evaluation is both formative and summative.

Evaluation drives instruction.

Evaluation views approximation as a demonstration of a learner's valid attempt to achieve the conventional form.

Evaluation uses learning logs, interviews, observations and careful examination of products as the evidence of student learning.

Evaluation reflects teacher's beliefs of what makes an effective learner.

Evaluation is driven by a set of pre-determined markers which are linked to the teacher's beliefs.

Evaluation should result in optimal learning for all those involved.

(Frameworks, 1991)

A discussion of these beliefs in small groups of parents and teachers made it patently clear that there could be no system of percentages, letter grades or percentiles which could convey to all those with a stake in the education process the mass of information about the individual child's growth and development as a learner.

It was agreed that a basic tenet should be that evaluation should give an accurate picture of what children can do, and help to set goals for the future. This 'picture' would provide parents with information about what they could expect from their children and allow them to see what had been achieved. Children also are boosted by seeing what they can do by having an attainable set of goals, and teachers have specific information with which they can plan work aimed at helping the children attain those goals.

3. Range of reporting options

To demonstrate in a practical manner how all the above could be achieved without resorting to the traditional measuring instruments, a range of formats and strategies was presented to parents to demonstrate the richness and relevance of the data that could be obtained. Some examples are presented below: a product evaluation applied to a piece of writing from a five-year-old Kindergarten student and two self-evaluations.

Product evaluation

In the product evaluation the format used is a comprehensive one developed to focus on what the student can do in writing, what skills and processes have been developed, so that future directions and demonstrations can be determined which are relevant to the individual and the group. It was first developed by a group of teachers in my past school (Warrawong School). Figure 9.4 shows the range of possible criteria which can be used to evaluate a piece of writing whether the writer be five or twelve years of age.

Jane is a five-year-old Kindergarten girl. She wrote the piece shown below about a birthday party she was about to have. The piece is a first draft. The product evaluation shows the processes that Jane has undertaken to complete the writing. It focuses on the meaning she has been able to express, the types of structures she has employed, the conventions over which she has gained, or is gaining control, the strategies that she has used to assist in gaining this control and other additional information that has been gathered from this exercise. Her immediate and long term needs are noted and actions for the future are specified. When eight of these product evaluations are applied to pieces of writing over the period of a year a tremendously rich and detailed picture of the student's development as a writer is presented. How much more useful to all concerned than a series of numerical or letter grades? The parents agreed wholeheartedly.

I am having my birthday at my house heps of chilljn are cuming to it it will be fun there will Be a Big cloon My Grandad is the cloon He will be fune cloon.

NAME:		TEXT: (Child's own choice of topic OR set topic. e.g. read and retell)		DATE:

Meaning	Structure	Conventions		Additional Information
		Punctuation/ Grammar	**Spelling**	
• Is it clear? • Does it make sense? • Is the main idea developed? • Is sufficient informatin provided? • Does it need tightening? • Does it show recognition of audience? (e.g. proper nouns vs pronouns) • Does it show an understanding of purpose (to explain, describe, argue, persuade, inform?)	• Syntax • Sequence • Appropriateness of lead and ending • Is the writing cohesive? • Are there guiding structures? e.g. title, headings, subheadings, labelled diagrams	• capitals • full stops • commas • apostrophes • quotation marks • hyphens • dashes • colons • semicolons • exclamation marks • underlining • tense • parts of speech • singular/plural	• using letter sounds and names • using the way it feels to speak • using their own idiosyncratic pronunciations • using their visual memory • using their kinaesthetic memory • using analogy • using their knowledge of the meanings conveyed by the letter clusters they see in spelling • using authoritative sources • using mnemonics • using guessing and confirmation (from 'Writing K-12' N.S.W. Department of School Education)	• length of piece compared with previous samples • register • displayed knowledge of concepts • evidence of spillover from other language experiences, e.g. reading, HSIE and S & T • suitability of the vocabulary/learning to the register • use of reference material • comprehension of text (read and retell) • overt r/w behaviour • ability to reconstruct text • handwriting • attitudes, e.g. willingness to 'have a go'

OBSERVED NEEDS:	What is the child's immediate need which I should address? (Observed needs should form the basis of the class program.)

Figure 9.4: Product evaluation frame

NAME: Jane Acton		TEXT: My Birthday party		DATE: August 9, 1992
Meaning	**Structure**	**Conventions**		**Additional Information**
• Composed text to express her own idea about her birthday party using – – environmental print – letter sounds – memory • Meaning is very clear • Information is provided to the reader • Purpose is achieved – audience is informed	• Used one continuous sentence • Endeavored to separate thoughts into sentences by use of capital letters often in the correct place • Used a good lead and ending • Story well sequenced	**Punctuation/ Grammar** • Used full stop correctly at the end of the sentence • Used capital letters appropriately • Used same tense throughout the piece • Used auxilliary verbs correctly • Good grasp of singular and plural	**Spelling** • Copied environmental print e.g. 'birthday', 'house', 'Grandad' • Used letter sounds e.g. 'heps', 'heaps' • Using the way it feels to speak e.g. 'Chiljn' – 'Children' • Used memory e.g. 'I am having my…' '…it will be fun…' '…there will be…' • Used guessing and confirming	• Length of piece consistent with stage of development and previous efforts • Spillover obvious from other language and curriculum experiences • Obvious risktaker – not afraid to use vocabulary with which she is not familiar • Used language appropriate to experiences • Has reconstructed demonstrated text types • Has comprehended other texts and has been able to model from these
OBSERVED NEEDS: • Continued immersions in print of all types • Planned demonstration in both reading and writing→constructing shorter sentences – eliminating overuse of "and"				

Figure 9.5 Product evaluation – Jane

Self-evaluation

I have included two examples of students' efforts at self-evaluation. Again rich data are revealed here by having the students recognise the importance of their perception of self as a learner. By working in a co-operative collaborative manner with their teachers they have come to many marvellous conclusions about the relevance and purpose of their schooling. They value their place in the curriculum as negotiated between teacher and student and have been able to skilfully assess their strengths and weaknesses and their successes in the learning process.

SELF-EVALUATION OF MISTY G. – YEAR 6

Attitudes

I think differently towards other people now that I have worked with different people. I am concerned about the environment and I care for it a lot more. I am a lot more honest and I share my belongings. I can take on a task and finish it without the teacher nagging me. My self-esteem has developed more. I feel more confident about myself.

Skills

I have improved in art by practising to draw trees, flowers and leaves. I have improved in maths. I can realistically write longer stories and read longer, because of silent reading. I can talk and listen better because of the peer support program. My dance and drama skills have improved, because of the program we did on dance and drama.

Physical

I have grown a lot in the past year. I am taller. I have bigger feet. I have longer legs, longer hair. I am more mature about the way I present myself. The oils in my skin have started to go crazy and I am starting to get pimples. I am starting to get bigger hips so I look fatter.

Teacher's comment

Misty is a mature, sensible and reliable young woman. She can be trusted to complete a task, properly, without supervision. She has a warm sense of humor and the ability to be tactful. Misty volunteers to help, is co-operative and is developing into an excellent leader. If Misty perseveres with her studies, tries as hard as she does now, she will do very well in any career she chooses. A pleasure to work with, indeed.
V.M. Teacher

SELF-EVALUATION OF LISA: YEAR 5

How I think and feel about …

Myself:

I am happy about who I am because I can do lots of things and I am more confident about myself.

Myself and others:

I think that I play with sensible friends because they don't do stupid things or get me into trouble. I love my family very much. I feel I don't get along with my brother. I also feel I get along with girls better than boys.

Myself and my school:
I have two wonderful teachers. They don't scream at me only if I'm talking. I like the fun things they give us to do.

I have learnt how to …
I have learnt how to be a better Goal Defence in netball. I have learnt how to play a keyboard. I have also learnt a lot about art with Mrs M. I have also learnt how I can help the environment.

I would like to learn more about …
I would like to learn more about artists and famous people. I would also like to learn more about the environment and what I can do to help it. I would also like to learn more about countries and cities.

I have enjoyed …
I have enjoyed being on the netball team and being in a double class with two excellent teachers and learning how to play the keyboard. I have also enjoyed working with other people. I am looking forward to the sports carnival.

Teacher's comments:
Lisa is an enthusiastic and dedicated young lady who is achieving excellent results in many areas. She has formed strong friendship bonds and works well in group situations. Although she completes her work as required she often chooses not to share with a large group.
Lisa has demonstrated control in the area of writing and reading. Her writing is clear and her editing skills are developing well. She enjoys participating in Visual Art activities and has improved her drawing skills. Well done!
Miss G.

These two comprehensive self-evaluations were obtained from their students by two valued and respected colleagues as a model to share with the teachers and parents. They provided a marvellous profile of the students' learning experiences and achievements over a period of a year.

Teachers and parents were 'sold' on the alternative options for evaluation. Using models from colleagues at other schools provided us with very useful demonstrations of what we could do in our school, as well as providing us with an understanding as to why these procedures were more useful than the traditional grades, percentages and other measurement based forms of reporting which the school had generally been using up until this point.

PHASE 4: MOVING ON ...

The remainder of the year saw the same process repeated. Issues were discussed by the committee. Recommendations from the committee were made to the staff. These were again discussed and either accepted or returned to the committee to consider the concerns of individuals or groups. Parents were advised and involved in the entire process and their continued contributions were welcomed and valued. We believed that the full participation of parents in this developmental process was instrumental in the success of the project. Without their awareness, involvement and support through increased knowledge, there can be no success. And we found that this support is exactly what we received from them. At the end of the first year a survey of parents and staff was undertaken. The results below were not spectacular, but were encouraging enough for us to carry on. There were sufficient encouraging signs amongst the figures and comments to make us believe that there was informed support from the staff and parents for the deep beliefs that we, the committee, held.

The suggestions from both staff and parents were noted and formed the basis of the evaluation procedures to be trialled in the following year.

PARENT SURVEY RESULTS
There were 133 responses:
69% were positive
21% wished for the inclusion of a comparison
10% preferred a grading system

All responses indicated they would like a written report
All except 2 are confident in requesting interviews
All responses saw value in interviews
All except 1 understood 1991 report

RESULTS OF INTERVIEWS AND WRITTEN REPORTS IN COMBINATION:

Number of Responses	Preference
34	2 interviews and 2 reports
21	Flexible interviews and 2 reports
10	Flexible interviews and 1 report
11	Interviews each term and 2 reports
11	1 interview and 2 reports

TEACHER SURVEY RESULTS

Suggestions for report form:
- eliminate lines from strands
- tick boxes for some areas
- more space for English
- scrap report form
- have a blank page

Suggestions for evaluation reporting procedures:
- more frequent interviews with a short report at the end of the year
- more frequent interviews with a report earlier in the year
- more frequent interviews with written report of what was said
- twice yearly interviews and written reports in tick form

Considerations:
- frequency of interviews and written reports
- form of reports
- disk access to written form
- flexibility

The results of the teacher survey also included encouraging signs and constructive suggestions.

PHASE 5: A NEW YEAR BEGINS

The direction taken for the following year strongly reflected these summaries.

It was a most exciting and challenging year which saw staff and parents struggle to come to grips with, and obtain maximum benefit from, evaluation procedures which were developed to reflect the changing beliefs of both groups.

Written communications (the old report card's new name) were provided to parents according to a new flexible formula designed to accommodate the needs and wishes of all stakeholders. They were basically of narrative style but flexibility was built in to enable those teachers who wished to devise a format to suit their own purposes to do so. To encourage such initiative, and also to monitor these developments, I devised and produced these adaptations of the written communication on the Macintosh computer. These often took the form of checklists formulated by individuals to enable clear communication. (All staff quickly came to the realisation that the only relevant and appropriate checklist was one developed by the individual teacher to accommodate his/her own needs, and those of his/her students.)

At the conclusion of 1992 another survey of staff and parents was administered. The results this time were quite spectacular, revealing an incredibly increased awareness among both staff and community of the purposes and procedures involved in student evaluation. If the categories 'adequate', 'successful' and 'extremely successful' can be considered to be supportive of the procedures the results of the survey revealed overwhelming parental support.

SURVEY
NOVEMBER
1992

INTERVIEWS

1. Sharing information
   about your child
                   0   0   11 **51-0**   4   36

2. Understanding many
   aspects of your child's
   progress
                   0   0   11 **50-0**   3   36

3. Becoming more
   aware of your child's
   needs
                   0   3   15 **50-3**   5   30

4. Feeling more able to
   help and support your
   child's learning
                   0   3   11 **50-3**   9   30

WRITTEN COMMUNICATIONS

1. Support information
   exchanges at the
   interview
                   1   2   12 **51-3**   7   32

2. Inform you as to your
   child's progress
                   2   2   10 **49-4**   7   32

3. Your opinion of its
   format and
   presentation
                   2   2   17 **49-4**   8   24

4. How satisfied with the
   flexibility
                   0   0   9 **53-0**   5   39

Figure 9.6: Survey results at the end of the second year

PHASE 6: AND STILL WE ARE GOING

As a result of this, staff and parents decided early in 1993 to continue the development of the formats and procedures in an effort to ensure that student evaluation reflected beliefs, classroom strategies and curriculum goals and at the same time provided all stakeholders with the information they required in the format which was of the greatest value and provided the most usable information.

Parents were asked to provide written comments as part of the evaluation survey and just a few of these are included to demonstrate the acceptance and enthusiasm with which the evaluation policy was greeted.

I was very happy with the format and organisation of the interview. I don't know of any improvement that could be made (to written communications). As my child is in her first year at school, the interviews are new to me but on both occasions I have had an interview I felt that the teacher covered all aspects of my daughter's progress and I found her very easy to talk to. The idea of having interviews is excellent as parents know that if they are having any problems or their children are having any problems they can be discussed in the interview at not only the teacher's request but also the parent's request. I appreciated the teacher taking time to talk to me and making me feel that I can do so at any time.

Interviews: more flexible hours, possibly evenings to cater for working parents enabling both parents to attend together instead of 'mum' reporting back to 'dad'. I am happy with the way the written communication is being carried out so far. I feel that it gives more detailed description of my children's progress, strengths and weaknesses. I would like to add that I appreciate the long hours and dedication involved in preparing the written reports for each individual child, and that I feel that my child's teachers really 'know' my children after reading them. They are much more personal than the old method of ticking the appropriate column. Thank you.

Interviews — as early in the year as possible so problems can be dealt with quickly. Be as specific in (written) comments as possible. Don't be afraid to criticise children and request parental help with behavior problems. Perhaps if a problem is occurring with a child — be it behavioral or with school work — then if the teacher could contact the parent for an interview immediately or maybe phone, both the teacher and parent could work together for the child's benefit and in the end it would also benefit the other pupils in the class. In the past, speaking from experience, the parent has not been contacted until a minor problem has become a major problem.

CONCLUSION

Arthur L. Costa (1989) maintains that most schools lack a school-wide plan for collection and use of information, and that school staffs should constantly scrutinise the curriculum for alignment of curriculum goals, instructional strategies, and evaluation activities.

I have tried to suggest ways that the first of these objectives could be achieved by providing a description of the processes followed by one school in empowering staff and parents through involvement, and supporting their endeavors to overcome problems and concerns to achieve a result which greatly benefited both. I have also touched on the second part of the quotation in briefly describing a few of the methods, formats and strategies used to bring about that vital 'alignment'.

Evaluation of student achievement and program effectiveness are the keystones of the success of our educational endeavors. There must be involvement and ownership in the development of these programs and policies for them to be relevant and successful. They must apply across the curriculum in all its aspects and implications. Evaluation must look at the whole child in all of his/her educational endeavors, not just those elements that can be measured by clinical instruments. Test scores represent only a small part of the total information picture.

The different audiences we provide for, and service, require different interpretations from the information that we have obtained about student achievement. This range of information is needed so that correct decisions can be made on future educational directions and actions. Decisions are constantly being made at various levels whether it is for an individual education plan for a student or a group of students, a school plan, a decision on district action, at state or even national level. Teachers make daily instructional decisions based on their data collection and interpretation of the child and the classroom. Principals will make decisions based on the knowledge gained from staff, students, community, media, politicians and senior system personnel (cluster directors, superintendents, supervisors, etc.), while still accommodating and abiding by local, state and national policies, guidelines and laws. Given relevant, rigorous information, in a format appropriate to the particular audience, hopefully decision makers will take a holistic view and arrive at educational decisions rather than those which are administrative and/or expedient.

Staff and parents must have full ownership of the project and full support, protection and encouragement must be constantly afforded to them. The assistance of outside personnel, including university undergraduate and post graduate students, lecturers and system personnel, is vital. If this can be incorporated into the total policy, enabling teaching staff to be researchers and co-researchers with others, the outcomes are more relevant and durable and therefore more likely to be accepted and embraced by all stakeholders.

Our commitment to establishing relevant, meaningful and 'do-able' evaluation procedures is very strong. These should not merely result in the accumulation and recording of data but must lead to more efficient teaching and learning. Evaluation should be quick, easy, useful and it should be the basis of relevant policies formulated through need determined by the evaluation process. This, in turn, is responsible for increased skills, knowledge and understandings for all concerned, promoting improved attitudes and the implementation of more appropriate strategies. This completes the cycle and the result is better, more meaningful, more enjoyable and more relevant programs which are supported, understood and appreciated by all parties in the process.

10

Collaborating on assessment

Changing the culture of assessment and evaluation

by Stan Warren

Stan Warren tells the story of a co-researching project involving teachers, parents, and the local cluster director that gradually and dramatically changed the culture of evaluation and co-operation that had existed in his school for many years. Stan admits to having had fairly traditional views on the role and nature of evaluation in schools but when, as a newly appointed principal to a school servicing children of upwardly mobile, highly educated and articulate parents, his views were challenged, his resultant intellectual unrest sowed the seeds for the project.
For those of you who are concerned about how to pull the parents along with you as you try to develop evaluation strategies that result in 'optimal learning for all', Stan's chapter will provide some useful ideas.

BACKGROUND

When I became principal of Nareena Hills Public School in 1987 I found a school characterised by a highly articulate community that held strong traditional views of evaluation. The prevailing view amongst the parents was one which valued lock-step progress through school from grade to grade as the only way successful learning could be recognised. The way to evaluate learning (so these parents believed) was to test students on standardised and teacher-set instruments to provide a ranked order of the students. The winners were always the winners and others were seen as trying hard to give their best effort.

This view was in conflict with the statewide policy to introduce an outcomes-based model of education and an outcomes standards framework for evaluating student learning. The move towards outcomes-based education implied that teachers, parents and students needed to reach consensus on what authentic or 'good' learning was. The outcomes-based model that NSW had implemented insisted firstly that it was necessary to view all learners as being capable of success, and secondly that there was no necessity for all learners to come to a predetermined outcome at a predetermined point in the process. Rather, the model states that each learner should be guided to each outcome over time. This implies a view of the learner as an individual with unique learning interests, experiences and background who is involved in the process of learning new things. It strongly suggests that it would be inappropriate to view learners in terms of their ranked position in a total group.

Another message from the outcomes set out in the NSW K-6 English syllabus is that learning is an ongoing process involving much more than traditional views encapsulated by a lock-step, back-to-basics philosophy. I interpreted the main message in this syllabus to be:

It is not good enough to make decisions about learners of any age on the basis of one evaluative experience which is carried out on one particular day, and then summarise this experience as a number or a grade.

As principal, I was uneasy about this situation. I had always seen one of my roles as demonstrating to the school community that the monitoring of learning across the grades is efficient and directed. To do this I believed that it was necessary to collect and store information that could be used to demonstrate where each child fits into the grade and the progress being achieved. Being new to the school, I was keen to demonstrate my commitment to effective teaching and learning and I wanted to ensure that the activities happening in classrooms were well planned, effectively implemented and conscientiously monitored for each individual child. As well as that, I was keen to ensure that the processes for reporting progress were rigorous and 'modern'. I wanted teachers to involve students in their own evaluation and parents to feel that they could make input to the decisions and ask questions about what their child was doing.

I also wanted students to be confident that they could reach their own potential without fear of being compared to others in the group, BUT I also wanted to keep office records of progress in standardised tests to 'check' the progress. While the philosophy behind the outcomes in the syllabus was causing me some mild intellectual unrest, I seemed to be able to deal with it until one member of staff asked 'Why are we doing this?'. She was referring to the eclectic mixture of assessment and evaluation procedures I had put into place in the school.

THE BEGINNINGS OF STRONG INTELLECTUAL UNREST

I was conscious of the need to empower teachers to implement processes that were consistent with the outcomes they were articulating for students. The teacher who asked me the 'Why are we doing this?' question got the predictable 'new principal' response which typically claims that '... it is in the interests of monitoring students' learning and my accountability to the clientele'.

This didn't satisfy this teacher. She continued to probe the issue by taking the results of the standardised tests that had been given to her class and placing them alongside the extensive qualitative records she kept of the children's progress. There was an obvious mismatch. The results for some children on the test were a clear support of the information gathered by the teacher, but for other children, the results did not demonstrate individual children's progress, nor did they represent the effort those children were making. I had to agree with the teacher's extensive information and it was clear that some children were being misrepresented in the test results. She went on to (gently) tell me that she was 'sick of setting homework sheets! It takes me hours to prepare it on Sunday afternoon, I take a lot of time to go through it on Monday, I get it back on Thursday and I feel pressured to get it back to the kids by Friday, so it takes over my teaching ... and I'm not convinced that it helps most children learn more effectively ... nor enjoy their learning!'

This started a huge process of reflection on what real learning was and how it could be effectively monitored and clearly communicated to the parents AND THE STUDENTS!

AFTER THE UNREST: ACTION!

I've discovered that strong intellectual unrest leads to action. This teacher's questions and the introduction of an outcomes standards framework led me to talk with other teachers about why they were doing certain things. These discussions raised a number of questions that I realised I needed to address:
- How did assessment/reporting procedures reflect what was happening in classrooms?
- How could parents be led to understand what learning was really about?
- How did testing help the teacher to understand the child's progress?

- What did the external tests add to the parent's/teacher's understanding of the child?
- Did the results of all tests need to be interpreted 'in context' so parents could have a more precise understanding of their child's learning?
- What information did parents already have about their child's learning/progress?
- How did the parents respond to the teacher's evaluation of the child's progress?
- How could all this information be made useful to ensure the child's progress and maintain his/her self-esteem as a learner?

With those questions in mind I initiated a parent meeting to discuss evaluation, reporting and the needs of students, parents and teachers. An outcome of this meeting was the project outlined below.

THE PROJECT BEGINS

As a consequence of the meeting, we agreed on some collaborative research. The broad aim of the project was to implement an evaluation plan that would address the needs of all stakeholders and to involve each of them in the process. All left the meeting with a strong belief that each of the stakeholders could add data that would influence the understanding of the outcome.

The teachers decided to investigate continuous anecdotal evaluation and reporting to parents. The parents, however, were dubious that this innovation was realistic and indicative of individual students' school success because they had mostly experienced fairly traditional forms of education and wanted to retain their children in the same/similar mode. It was something they understood, and with all the dynamic changes occurring in the curriculum area, it was one thing they wanted to hang on to. The problem as I saw it was to develop an authentic assessment/evaluation/reporting system that was fair to all students and easily understood by all involved.

An academic friend directed me to a chapter from a book by Anthony et al. (1991) which set out a model of literacy evaluation that looked at the role of student, teacher and parent. The ideas were similar to the things that my teachers had been trying so I distributed it to them. One, a teacher of a composite class, came to seek my support in implementing what she had read in the article. She proved to be what Roy Williams (Chapter 9) called his 'platform for success'.

This teacher wanted to implement a process of assessment and reporting that would keep the focus firmly on individual students. Her process can be summarised thus:

- She decided to take and keep extensive anecdotal records.

- She decided to continuously update parents' information on the progress of their children.
- Her plan was to focus on six students per week and spend time on Friday afternoons writing a brief summary report on each of these six students and sending it home. This meant that each child in the group could have a written evaluation statement every five weeks.

I adopted the role of co-researcher and took on the job of gathering potential formats for recording and communicating the information gathered.

I also took opportunities to observe her students at work. This provided the teacher with opportunities to explore ideas with me, to try out ideas for new approaches and to suggest ways of describing what she was observing. We initiated debriefing sessions on a weekly basis so we could tease out our working knowledge of each student in the class. This meant that as the written statements were drafted there was agreement on the descriptors being used to explain the children's progress.

While the project was developing, other teachers were watching the change with great interest. Within the first five weeks or so two other teachers approached me to become involved. They indicated that the work being done was in line with their beliefs about teaching and learning and were keen to trial the approach in a parallel class.

Each of the teachers collected anecdotal data on five or six students each week. The focus was aimed across the curriculum and a sheet was drawn up for each student. The teacher recorded observations according to the objectives set in the program in English and mathematics particularly. A third area was set aside on the sheet where general comments about the child's engagement in other areas of the curriculum could be noted.

THINGS I NOTICED THIS WEEK: Week Beginning _____

ENGLISH

MATHEMATICS

GENERAL COMMENTS (including other curriculum areas):

Figure 10.1: Sample recording sheet

In the beginning, each teacher only recorded specific responses to the strategies being used. It was not for some time that confidence grew to the stage that the teachers were willing to describe their perception of the level at which the child was working. Indicators of this nature were difficult to determine but as parents became more familiar with the procedures, and as their confidence in the teacher's understanding of their child grew, they began to ask more informed questions of the child's learning.

CHANGING THE EVALUATION CULTURE OF PARENTS

Although my parent community was a highly articulate and confident one, like parents from other schools I had worked in, many were not confident about approaching the school to engage in discussion about their children's learning. Over the past decade a good deal has been written about the need to involve parents more in the decision-making that affects their particular child's education. Most of this literature agrees that parents and teachers have fostered the view that the professionals should carry the responsibility for the learning achieved by all students. By the same token, the view that parents are the child's first educator has gradually begun to influence this kind of thinking. There is evidence emerging to demonstrate that children's learning is fostered when the parent works together with the teacher for the benefit of the child — in fact when all three work together in a positive and supportive situation, the progress of students is considerably enhanced.

One part of the project was to get parents to write down what they already knew of their children's learning progress. In each reporting period a survey was sent to the parents to get them to tell the school about what they knew of their children's learning. We focused on the child as a writer, as a reader, as a mathematician, and on other areas of the curriculum. This was a dynamic part of the reporting process because we wanted the parents to learn more about how their children learned and the indicators that demonstrated that progress was being made.

While this move was successful in getting parents involved, there was still strong doubt that what we were attempting was valuable. Some parents were still being judgemental about the teaching/learning processes that were being employed and were unhappy with the focused evaluation and reporting the teachers were doing. I decided this could be overcome if parents could 'see' their children in learning situations. The problem was how to arrange this so that the majority of parents could be involved.

One strategy that was very successful was tied to a school development day. At that time in the NSW system schools were able to use two days per year for staff development activities. It was decided that we would work on one of these days in the area of student evaluation. We invited our cluster director to come to the school to work with us. He agreed to teach three demonstration lessons that we could video and then use as the focus for the development day (the next day). The plan was to focus on the markers we were using in our assessment strategies and he encouraged us to invite the parents into the exercise so they would have the opportunity to see the classes in action and be able to join the discussion the next day.

On the development day we discovered that reflecting on the reactions of the students during each of the lessons was particularly valuable. In one situation, one of the students appeared to be totally uninterested in the lesson in progress. He physically moved himself to the edge of the group and became distracted by a toy on a desk nearby. His mother asked if he was often like this. His teacher explained that it was always in his best interests to constantly redirect the student's attention to the task in hand. The mother commented that she had noticed similar behavior at home when they were doing things as a family.

While the child was looking at the toy, the teacher on the video (the cluster director) asked a question that the child obviously recognised. Without thinking, and without removing his focus from the toy in his hand, he gave an appropriate answer. The teacher probed further and the child clearly demonstrated that he had been engaged in the lesson and that he had a working knowledge of the topic. What did this demonstrate? What did we learn of the child's learning in this situation? How could we capitalise on it for the future learning of the child?

WHAT DID THIS MEAN FOR THE SCHOOL CULTURE OF EVALUATION AND COLLABORATION?

The discussion that arose at the development day was another 'platform for success'. Together the teachers and parents were able to analyse the video, talk to the cluster director about what he was trying to do in the demonstration lesson, and his perception of the child's responses to the lesson strategies. This collaborative interaction was highly valued by teachers and parents alike, as a stronger bond of trust and understanding began to develop. Both parents and teachers indicated they felt happier about working more closely in the child's interests because some of the old barriers had been broken down.

One thing that emerged was a reinforcement of the valuable role trust plays in the teaching/learning situation. If a parent is openly judgemental of the teacher, or vice versa, the student's learning is disadvantaged. On many occasions parents have been known to discuss the teaching and learning in a school in a most destructive manner. When the intent of their remarks has been heard by the teachers, the element of trust and co-operation is devalued and it takes a long time to re-establish the communication. At the same time, many school staffrooms echo with teachers' views of the parents that form the school clientele. This also is unhealthy and needs to be treated with caution, as the students' learning may ultimately be the loser.

It is interesting that, in this particular school, those teachers whose children are also students here say they try really hard not to talk about their children in the school setting 'in case they are disadvantaged'. Isn't it an enigma that in a learning environment built on trust and support, the main players in the game relax into the attitude they would most like to break down in the wider community?

EXTENDING THE PROJECT

During the time we were developing and refining our approach to assess-ment and reporting, the issue of decreasing enrolment became of increasing concern and led to the need for more composite classes. The difference between the parents' view of composite classes and the teachers' view was widening. The school council was involved in all discussions on the most appropriate way to structure classes across the school, and inevitably some parents and teachers were happy while others were concerned about the progress students would make. That year we built on the trust that had been developing to structure a situation that would help to break down the view that composite classes were detrimental to learning.

We structured the classes in such a way that all students were able to retain daily contact with their age-cohort, to be streamed (according to acceptable indicators) in one area of the curriculum so they could work with other students who were exhibiting similar characteristics, regardless of age, and also to have the opportunity to be stimulated in a selected group for a period of about ten weeks (one term).

This was a very radical change from any organisation used previously and it was imperative that it 'worked' from the outset. There was a need for the teachers to be enthusiastic and positive about the innovation and to prove its value and success in every situation. The strongest need for the students was to increase each one's self-esteem within their age-cohort and to break down any sense of competitiveness that was interfering in their learning attitudes. We decided to do this by holding grade meetings for 45 minutes at the beginning of the day when the focus of the teaching would be on personal development, health and physical education. It was our intention to focus mainly on group activities and to establish a collaborative and accepting environment across the school community.

During the next hour of each day the students were regrouped into eight classes for mathematics. However, we decided to ignore the age level of the students and to place them into groups according to the levels described in the Australian National Profile for Mathematics. It was agreed by the staff that we should take the first five weeks of the year to make an intensive assessment of the skills and understandings already achieved by each student and place them into a group that would lead them on to the next level. The teachers would structure a program that would hold this concept as its main aim. While negotiating the groups, a good deal of discussion focused on the self-esteem of the learners and the impact the regrouping may have, particularly if the older students needed to be grouped in lower levels. The outcome was that the teachers agreed to continue to teach in groups and to maintain, as much as possible, a similarity of age within each group.

At the end of the evaluation program it was clear that this issue was not as problematic as was first thought. However, the other aspect of the organisation that simplified the task was the fact that in planning the innovation there was agreement among the staff that one full-time teacher should be retained class-free during this period of the day. That person was given the responsibility of team-teaching across the school in response to the needs of students in each of the groups. The teacher of the group would identify the needs of students and then invite support from the class-free teacher. The use of the staff in such a flexible way meant the students' learning could be catered for in a more focused manner and the collaboration between the teachers was greatly enhanced. Evaluation was also more refined, in that the teachers were able to share their impressions of the students at work, and focus on the products of the work to form a more complete view of the learning that was occurring.

The rest of the day was structured in seven grade-equivalent classes so the students could experience the five other key learning areas in the primary school curriculum. The other two members of staff were involved in an open-plan, team-teaching class of about 55 students selected from grades by the grade-supervisor on criteria set in negotiation with the whole staff. The students went to the group for 10 weeks (one term) and then returned to the grade and a different group was nominated according to different criteria. Again, this flexibility enabled the students to be challenged according to their particular needs and interests.

In keeping with the whole-school nature of this development, the teachers agreed to collaborate more closely on the units they would teach. The two teachers in the open-plan situation needed to be aware of what the grade teachers were presenting, and made a commitment to draw generalisations from across the grades to ensure that there was a reflection of the various units being taught embedded in what was presented to the students in the open-plan setting.

Collegiality was crucial to the success of this aspect of the work. The level of collaboration was high and the students were able to recognise the relationship of the work they were doing to the work being done in other classes. The teachers took the time to make what they were doing explicit to the students, and it was heartening to hear the students sharing the work they were doing in informal situations and inviting each other to visit their classroom to see the various aspects of the work. Teachers, too, took the time to find out what others were doing in their particular classroom and this greatly enhanced the environment of the school as one of learning, collaboration and support.

SOME OUTCOMES OF THE PROJECT

The feedback from parents was encouraging. Many were excited that their students were enthusiastically sharing the activities they were doing at school when they arrived home. The students were able to articulate both the organisation in which they were involved as well as the learning they were achieving. Parents were always encouraged to visit the classrooms and see, first-hand, the learning process in action. As a consequence teachers and parents began to develop a more supportive view of each other and the curriculum the child was experiencing.

This need for a positive relationship between parents and teachers can never be underestimated. Each has to retain an open and honest trust in the other to ensure the child reaches the optimal outcomes desired by both.

It was heartening to receive feedback from parents whose children had gone on to high schools where assessment and evaluation is typically more traditional. These parents reported that they were more prepared to ask questions about evaluation from an informed base outside the classroom. This in turn had created a need for high school teachers to be more closely attuned to the nature of the external experiences on children's assessment and evaluation.

CONCLUSION

Learning can never be viewed in a vacuum. Children are highly interactive beings who are constantly changing. They are subject to a far wider range of stimuli than ever in the past. Parents and teachers need to recognise the changing nature of the world, the changing nature of information and facts, and embrace the fact that teaching needs to change to accommodate the needs, interests and abilities of students in a far more complex society. If we agree with the fact that the parent is the child's first teacher, it cannot be denied that the parent has a good deal to add to the perceptions of the child as a learner. When parents and teachers co-operate and perhaps agree to invite the child to share all aspects of the evaluation process, the potential for optimal learning for all will be greatly enhanced.

11

Teacher empowerment

Evaluation in the hands of teachers

by John Bladen

Senior departmental administrators also have important roles to play in the management of schools and, like principals, they sometimes have to walk a very thin line between the expectations of the department they represent and the schools for which they are expected to provide educational leadership and support. In this chapter John Bladen, a cluster director within the NSW Department of School Education, describes how he provided leadership for his schools when outcomes-based education became departmental policy which he had to help his schools understand and implement. First he addresses the concept of 'accountability' Then he describes how he 'got his hands dirty' in order to understand what the implications of outcomes-based education for assessment and evaluation were.

CONTEXT

The development of outcomes-based education has raised questions about the role of the classroom teacher in assessing student growth and development. Are teachers truly capable of making valid judgements about student achievement of educational outcomes? Do external measures provide more reliable data, more readily aggregated to provide systemic information? Can all stakeholders in a child's education be assured that evaluation in the hands of teachers is rigorous, valid and authentic?

The reality is that teachers make professional judgements about student growth and development every day. Through daily interaction and reflection, teachers become instruments of a continuous evaluation process in which student needs, responses, attitudes, and developing skills and knowledge are assessed and evaluated for the purpose of providing optimal learning. Whether such energy is perceived to satisfy the demands of accountability is a vexed question which impacts on schools and educational systems nationally and internationally.

Meeting the demands of accountability involves three distinct aspects. Teachers being directly accountable to students and parents involves **moral accountability**. Being accountable to professional standards and norms involves **professional accountability**, and being accountable to government involves **contractual accountability**. All three forms require that teachers be able to provide an account of their activity and work for the relevant audiences.

Moral accountability requires direct communication of information to students and parents based on cumulative professional judgements frequently made in partnership with students themselves. The development of national profile statements and learning outcomes statements across state and national boundaries provides teachers with descriptive statements of standards to guide their professional judgements about student growth and development with attention to student learning processes; judgements still made in partnership with key stakeholders.

Professional accountability requires provision of an account to the body responsible for standards and norms of teaching and learning processes. The development of best practices statements provides teachers with a framework to discuss professional standards against agreed optimal practice. As shared understandings about what constitutes best practices, develop so best practices statements will begin to underpin school and individual teacher accountability and development mechanisms.

Contractual accountability requires those responsible in government to be able to provide information that gives an account of the performance and activity of individual schools and the system as a whole. Many educational systems have relied heavily on decontextualised measures of student achievement to provide performance information, resulting in a consequent narrowing of focus which has impacted on the power of the teacher to make professional judgements about student growth and development. In the face of external measures, teachers' professional judgements have frequently been sublimated to the perceived rigor of 'hard' externally gathered data.

TEACHER EMPOWERMENT

My involvement as co-researcher with Rosemary and Maureen in the application and development of responsive evaluation during 1991 and 1992 provided an opportunity to explore the notion of teacher empowerment in student evaluation. At the time Rosemary was teaching a composite Year 1/2 class at Gwynneville Public School, while Maureen was teaching Year 4 at the same school. The suburb of Gwynneville is close to the central business district of Wollongong and accommodates a broad socio-economic and culturally diverse community.

At the urging of colleagues from our local university (who constantly affirm the importance of field work by educational administrators), I made an initial approach to principal (John) requesting his support in negotiating my involvement with two staff members to explore the notion of responsive evaluation. John's affirmation and support for his immediate supervisor to work closely and regularly with two staff members speaks volumes for his leadership. Supported by this culture, Rosemary and Maureen became my co-researchers in our investigation of beliefs about teaching and learning and the translation of these beliefs into practice.

In establishing a co-researcher relationship, we relied heavily on the work of Jan Hancock of the University of Wollongong for a theoretical framework which emphasised the open and frank exchange of information between both parties. (Hancock 1991) Our initial approach was to take copious field notes of what appeared to be happening in the classroom. Each observation session was followed by a discussion of what we thought was happening and what the field notes indicated was happening. Who was on task? Which student settled first? What processes were students using to assist their learning? What partnerships existed between students and how did these support or impede learning? These and myriad other questions emerged as we sat for almost an hour after each observation session.

To facilitate our role as co-researchers, Rosemary, Maureen and I negotiated an active partnership in the classroom, initially with role reversal, where I would lead a lesson and they would take field notes, and later through team teaching and group work. Each of us had found observation to be somewhat threatening, even though the focus was always on the students learning rather than the teacher's practice. Having spent my career in classrooms, I constantly felt uncomfortable taking a 'fly on the wall' approach to field notes. More questions were raised than answered. Seeing and listening alone could not provide the whole story when it came to research about teaching and learning. The methodology was simply too passive. I craved interaction and joint reflection with students to find out what they were thinking and what their perceptions were of what was going on.

As Rosemary and Maureen started to direct my observations and increasing interactions with individual and particular groups of students, so our understandings and articulation of student learning increased. Rather than trying to capture the story in field notes we found video to be far more enlightening for our reflections.

When following a particularly interactive shared reading and discussion on plants, Trent (Year 1) asked me to share his writing response. He asked if I had read all the stories he had written during the year and proceeded to walk me through his accumulated writings. As I shared his early attempts at making meaning, through single words to single sentences and most recently, multiple sentences, Trent reflected that he was getting better with his story writing because he was writing more now and he sometimes checked his spelling from words in earlier stories. He asked me how to spell the word 'garden'. Despite my entreaties that Trent 'have a go', he was insistent that I should help. Having observed Rosemary construct a word bank during the shared book lesson I was aware that 'garden' had been recorded along with other relevant 'plant' words. I suggested to Trent that the word 'garden' might be already written on a chart around the room. Equally insistent as before, Trent assured me that it wasn't. My response, asking him was he sure, prompted Trent to scan the walls where, almost to his amazement, he discovered the sought after word. With great aplomb Trent strode from his desk, pointed to the desired word and returned to his seat to continue writing. Throughout this time the video camera continued to capture the interaction between Trent and me.

When Rosemary, Maureen, and I sat down to analyse the replay we were sure that Trent was really developing as a reflective learner. He was aware of his progress and he could articulate some of his own markers of success. Was this the first time Trent had used environmental print to support his writing? We weren't sure but we knew it took a degree of teacher imperative to get him to take the next step. Supporting Trent to take more control of his own learning processes became a continuing focus for us.

As co-researchers we were gradually beginning to articulate signals or markers of learning in a collaborative environment. Our reflections entered a recurring phase where we started to increasingly question the relevance of actual learning episodes. Might paired writing and joint construction help some of our less confident writers? Are our teacher demonstrations sufficiently explicit? Eventually we started to articulate our core beliefs about learning and explore the congruence between these beliefs and the teaching and student assessment methods we were employing. Most importantly came the growing confidence in our judgements about student growth and development.

As Rosemary investigated a portfolio-based approach to student assessment, evidence of learning outcomes was increasingly evaluated through multiple perspectives. Video and audio tapes, work samples, drafts, anecdotal and observational records collectively validated judgements. Matched to increasingly descriptive student reports and close interaction with parents, responsive evaluation provided a powerful methodology to support our combined professional growth.

RESPONSIVE EVALUATION AND SYSTEM EXPECTATIONS

Responsive evaluation provides a framework for student evaluation which is both rigorous and valid. It is a methodology that empowers teachers to fulfil moral, professional and contractual expectations of accountability. It includes the development of shared beliefs about learning which translate into congruent teaching/learning methodologies. Further, the incorporation of student assessment strategies as an integral component of teaching/learning episodes and the development of shared 'markers' of learning ensures relevance and collaboration in support of student outcomes. It is through collaboration and reflection that teachers, students and parents/caregivers come to more complete understandings of student growth and development.

The challenge facing teachers and educational administrators is the incorporation of the three forms of accountability in ways which retain the primacy of the role of the classroom teacher in the evaluation of student learning outcomes. Where the emphasis on outcomes focuses more on knowledge to the detriment of processes and attitudes, the danger of a minimal competencies mindset emerges. The seductiveness of simplistic measures of student learning outcomes is only too well known. Is it not far simpler to assess a child's mastery of sound/symbol relationships than the processes a child uses in constructing meaning from a particular text?

Rexford Brown (1991) describes the need for education for thoughtfulness and creativity, a vital component virtually destroyed by restrictive teaching practices, pragmatically adapted to meet the contractual accountability demands of state and district testing regimes in many parts of the United States. Against this backdrop there is a universal cry for more analytical, reflective and responsive learners, able to adapt to changing social and work environments. Any imposition of a 'teaching for automaticity' approach matched by equally simplistic student evaluation methodologies will pre-dictably diminish the responsiveness demanded by the rapid pace of change.

PROFILE STATEMENTS AND RESPONSIVE EVALUATION: QUO VADIS?

The development of state and, in some cases, national profile statements are intended to provide teachers with a framework by which to analyse student development. In my job I get to know about both the pros and cons as teachers see them.

The type of concerns expressed by teachers about profile statements include the possibility of professional judgements being 'locked into' defined expectations, the possible omission of other valuable learning indicators, a lack of personal ownership and in some cases a sense of 'working backwards'.

Perceived benefits include a sharpening of a specific subject focus, implications for particular teaching learning strategies and the provision of indicators the teacher may have overlooked.

In essence I see profile statements as a valuable curriculum and evaluation resource, providing that teachers can equate their personal learning 'markers' with the broader outcomes statements provided.

The challenge for teachers, school leaders and administrators is to support teachers in aligning their personal markers of learning to the profiles to the extent that teachers take ownership and internalise the broader statements. However, some teachers may not have worked collaboratively in the past and the imperative for teamwork in the assimilation of profiles will be critical. Further, teachers who have developed in an era that emphasised theories of teaching rather than theories of learning will experience acute discomfort on entering an era which emphasises the need to address individual preferred learning styles. Appropriate staff development will be necessary if the best attributes of the profiles are going to be realised.

Responsive evaluation provides a methodology that gives increased confidence and skills to teachers, as professional accountability increases. The ability to articulate personal and corporate beliefs about learning which underpin teaching/learning and student evaluation practices will be vital to continued teacher empowerment, and in striving to meet the contractual accountability processes, the role of state testing programs must emerge as validating rather than sublimating teachers' professional judgements. An effective marriage of information derived from personalised and decontextualised sources is necessary to ensure that teachers respond creatively to students' learning needs. At its core, evaluation in the hands of teachers is an issue of quality teaching and learning.

12

Yes, but how do we make assessment and evaluation 'scientific'?

by Brian Cambourne, Jan Turbill and Dianne Dal Santo

In Chapter 3 we described our 'criteria of effective evaluation' thus:
• Assessment and evaluation must result in optimal learning for all involved.
• Assessment and evaluation must inform, support and justify teacher decision-making.
• Assessment and evaluation practices must reflect the theories of language, learning and literacy which guide our teaching.
• The findings which result from our assessment and evaluation practices must be valid, reliable and perceived to be rigorous by all who use them.

In this chapter we deal with the fourth criterion: 'The findings which result from our assessment and evaluation practices must be valid, reliable and perceived to be rigorous by all who use them.'

This criterion became an important one for us because it relates to the way that those to whom teachers are accountable regard the scientific worth of non-measurement-based evaluation procedures. Most members of the general public, especially parents, politicians, and educational administrators, display a strong sense of mistrust toward such evaluation procedures, and in this project we found that when teachers decided to make the transition from a measurement-based approach to a more qualitative approach many of them also experienced strong feelings of uneasiness. We believe that this mistrust and uneasiness stems from widely held doubts about the 'scientific' worth of qualitative methods of assessment and evaluation.

The reason for this relates to some of the notions we discussed in Chapter 2, in particular 'paradigm paralysis' and 'paradigm shift'. The prevailing paradigm of evaluating student learning is one that insists that such evaluation can only be 'valid' if it is 'measurement-based, objective and has a high degree of something called 'reliability'.

University courses such as Statistics 101 fuel this discomfort by implying that assessment and evaluation procedures which are not measurement based are subjective, biased, unreliable, soft or invalid. Unless those who make the shift to qualitative methods can demonstrate that these procedures are at least as 'scientific' as those which characterise measurement-based evaluation, then they typically experience resistance and sometimes hostility to models of evaluation such as responsive evaluation.

This sense of mistrust and uneasiness was reflected in the questions that our co-researchers asked of each other and their co-researching partners:

• How can I (you) be sure that what I'm (you're) doing isn't subjective or biased?
• What about objectivity?
• How can I (you) be sure that what I'm (you're) doing in the name of assessment and evaluation is rigorous, valid, reliable, accurate, fair etc.?
• Is it scientific?

Inherent in these questions are doubts about the so-called scientific respectability of non-measurement based approaches to assessment and evaluation. As a group we decided to respond to this issue by:

• developing some agreed upon working definitions of basic terms
• exploring the notions of 'objectivity' and 'subjectivity'
• developing a set of procedures and/or processes which would increase the 'scientific' status, value and worth of our assessment and evaluation findings
• clarifying some of the differences between traditional measurement-based approaches to assessment and evaluation and responsive evaluation
• becoming familiar with the language used to describe the similarities between traditional measurement-based approaches to assessment and evaluation and responsive evaluation

SOME WORKING DEFINITIONS OF BASIC TERMS

We found some confusion and misunderstanding about terms that we were continually using. Two such terms are 'validity' and 'reliability'.

For example, in our group of co-researchers those of us who had taken basic courses in statistics, measurement or research design typically used these terms in very specific, rather narrow ways, overlaying them with statistical and/or numerical overtones. The intellectual baggage we had picked up from our formal preservice studies had given many of us a certain kind of lens through which we unconsciously filtered our understanding of the whole domain of assessment and evaluation.

We thought we could address this problem by looking for more generic, dictionary-like definitions of these terms. We found the meanings expressed in general dictionaries such as The Macquarie Dictionary or Webster's New World Dictionary a useful starting place. The Macquarie defines valid as 'sound, just, or well founded; having force, weight, or cogency; authoritative'. It defines 'reliable' as 'that which may be relied on; trustworthy'. Webster defines 'validity' as '... well grounded in principles or evidence' while 'reliability' means '... that which can be relied upon; dependable, trustworthy'.

As we explored the implications of terms such as 'dependable', 'sound', 'well founded', 'trustworthy', 'well grounded in principles or evidence' we developed some new (for us anyway) insights which pushed further. We began to understand why teachers, parents, politicians, administrators, and the public in general became uneasy and uncomfortable with evaluation methods that were not based on the principles and assumptions of the measurement-based paradigm.

With the help of researchers and theorists such as Guba & Lincoln (1981, 1989), Lincoln and Guba (1985), Peshkin (1988), Schwandt (1989) and Rorty (1991) we began to understand that the language and concepts that measurement-based evaluators used to test the 'truth' of their findings simply could not (and should not) be applied to responsive evaluation, or any other model of evaluation which was essentially qualitative in nature. It would be like judging apples using a set of criteria that were derived from cabbages. Such terms as 'rigor', 'reliability', 'validity', 'objectivity' which are applied to measurement-based evaluation cannot be transferred to other more qualitative approaches without distorting the picture which results.

Does this mean that responsive evaluation and similar methods of inquiry cannot be considered 'scientific'? No! It simply means that a different set of terms which represent slightly different concepts must be used to test the merit and worth of evaluation methods which are different from the more traditional measurement-based model. Table 12.1 illustrates what we mean. It summarises what we found to be the essential similarities and differences between traditional measurement-based evaluation and responsive evaluation.

Comparing the language and concepts in this way enabled us understand what the differences between the two paradigms were. We decided that we would be more 'scientific' if we talked about our findings using this language. Therefore instead of trying to argue that our methods of collecting data were 'rigorous', we would declare them to be 'trustworthy'. Instead of claiming that our results had high 'internal validity' we would argue that our results had 'high credibility'. Instead of trying to argue that our findings had high

Term used by measurement-based evaluator	Issue, concern, question that term relates to	Term used by responsive evaluator
RIGOR How rigorous are my procedures?	How scientific have I been in my procedures?	TRUSTWORTHINESS How trustworthy is the data I have collected?
INTERNAL VALIDITY How closely do my data and my results resemble reading and writing in the real world?	How close are my findings to reality?	CREDIBILITY Have I collected data and represented my findings in ways that credibly represent the realities of the stakeholders?
EXTERNAL VALIDITY How generalisable is the reading and writing behavior I find in this context to other contexts?	Can my findings be applied to the real world of reading, writing, etc.?	APPLICABILITY or TRANSFERABILITY Can the inferences I draw about reading and writing behavior be applied or transferred to other quite different contexts?
RELIABILITY How consistent, predictable are my data and my results?	Will the data I collect under these conditions be consistent from time to time?	DEPENDABILITY Is there a clear trail from my data to my conclusions that could be used to 'audit' my findings? Are the inferences I made dependable?
OBJECTIVITY Are my results free of bias and subjectivity?	Neutrality: Have I reduced the sources of bias?	CONFIRMABILITY Are my data and findings confirmable from multiple sources?

Table 12.1: Comparing the paradigms

'external validity' we would refer to their 'applicability' or 'transferability'. Rather than describe our results as 'reliable' we would describe them as 'dependable, and instead of 'objectivity' we would be seeking to increase the 'confirmability' of our results.

EXPLORING THE NOTIONS OF 'OBJECTIVITY' AND 'SUBJECTIVITY'

We discovered that objectivity and subjectivity have been dominant criteria in deciding what's 'good' or 'bad' science and/or 'good' and 'bad' evaluation for many years. The underlying message from this literature could be summed up as *Objectivity is good; subjectivity is bad*.

When we tried to understand how and why such a message was so strong in both the professional and the wider community we came to this conclusion. Since the time of Newton, the potential of the kind of science he did for discovering something called the 'truth' has been held in such high regard that society seems to have been subtly indoctrinated about the role that objectivity plays in research. As a consequence, one belief that seems to have been readily accepted both within and outside of science is that the 'truth' can only be arrived at through a carefully controlled, unemotional, impersonal, detached and sceptical attitude to everything. This attitude is seen by many to represent objectivity in action. The stereotype of the cool, detached, objective, scientist (usually with a Sigmund Freud beard) unemotionally and 'scientifically' collecting and then weighing the evidence is one which is implicitly communicated in much of the literature we read. The attainment of this kind of objectivity is enhanced (so the argument goes) if the degree to which the investigator (i.e. the scientist) actually influences the outcomes of what he is researching is reduced as close to zero as possible. In the jargon of research design this is called *reducing the reactivity of the subjects*.

It isn't hard to understand how this particular view of objectivity has spilled over into the assessment and evaluation field. In their rush to be accorded the same high status that the so-called 'hard' physical sciences had attained, researchers and theorists from other fields of study unquestionably accepted much of what physical scientists who followed the Newtonian tradition believed were self-evident truths. Two of these axiomatic truths were particularly pervasive:

- The only way to 'get at' the truth which is 'out there' waiting to reveal itself is by implementing the same procedures and methods that scientists like Newton and those who followed him advocated. This became known as 'the scientific method' and involved concepts like 'objectivity', 'reliability', 'validity' 'reliability' and 'systematic control of variables'.
- The belief that accurate measurement is at the core of any scientific enterprise.

In the assessment and evaluation field this lust for objectivity was thought to be achieved by interposing some objective instrument (a test) between the tester and testee and then standardising the procedures of administration and interpretation. By doing this it was claimed that any prejudices or biases the investigator might have had would be eliminated and thus the desired degree of objectivity would be achieved.

As we delved into more recent writings in epistemology and philosophy of science we found that such claims simply did not stand up to scrutiny.

We realised that while certain safeguards like standardising the tester–testee relationship and context may reduce this interactivity between the tester and testee, interactivity itself can never be eliminated. Despite all the controls, a large amount will always remain, and it is not only fruitless to pretend that it is not there, it is also intellectually dishonest. Even under the most rigorous of standardisation procedures which have been most scrupulously applied, the questions on any test are, after all, posed by the test designer in accordance with some perspective he or she holds, and that perspective includes all the biases and prejudices that normally characterise him or her.

But it doesn't stop here. Test designers assume that there is only one correct meaning of any text (and a standardised test is after all a text) and that this meaning is inherent in the words and phrases that make up that text. This leads to another related assumption, namely that subjects will therefore interpret the items on any test exactly as the test designer intended. This in turn leads to another assumption — that the test designer will interpret the responses exactly as the respondents intended. We know that recent linguistic and psycholinguistic science denies this. Meaning is also in language users' heads, and is significantly affected by the sum total of their prior experiences and knowledge. No two people can ever interpret the same text in identical ways.

We came to realise that value-free, context-independent objectivity is a pipe-dream that psychometricians have been chasing unsuccessfully since the measurement movement began. The issue of objectivity in all human research activities (and assessment and evaluation is after all merely one of a number of possible forms of research activity) is summed up by this observation:

There is no guarantee that when information is collected from human subjects, by whatever method, that there will not be interaction between those subjects and the minds that determined what information to collect and how to collect it. (Krathwol, cited in Guba & Lincoln 1981, p.90)

We asked ourselves whether objectivity in the classical sense described above really mattered. We decided to look at this issue from a quite different perspective, namely, whether or not assessor–assessee interaction was such a bad thing anyway, particularly with respect to the assessment of learning something as complex and multidimensional as language and literacy. We found plenty of examples in ethnography, sociology, anthropology and investigative journalism which indicated that humans could be sensitive, reliable, trustworthy and credible instruments of data collection.

We began to consider what the human-as-instrument could do and compared it with what that the so-called 'objective' test could not do. We came to these conclusions:

- First, the human is a **responsive instrument**. It can respond to all the personal and environmental cues which exist in the assessment context.
- Second, it is **adaptable**. It can collect information about multiple factors at multiple levels simultaneously.
- Third, it is **smart**. Like a smart bomb it can home in on information, change direction, run down leads, follow a trail, and ultimately hit the target. It can clarify, process, explore, summarise, triangulate on the spot, and do a host of other things that so-called 'objective', standardised instruments could never do. We concluded that it could cope with complexities much more effectively and quickly than any standardised test.

We realised that the complex nature of language behavior demands an instrument that can cope with such complexity and we came to the conclusion that the only instrument capable of doing all these things is the human mind. Rather than avoiding the interactions which students and the teachers who are trying to assess them are prone to, we realised that we should be exploiting them and maximising the richness and quality of data they can generate. We discovered that subjectivity as a source of bias and prejudice became a non-issue when certain credibility (i.e. rigorous in traditional language) procedures were used. Once we realised this we were able to explore a range of procedures which not only would increase the trustworthiness and credibility (i.e. validity and reliability in traditional language) of our findings but which would also ensure that bias, prejudice, and subjectivity could be significantly controlled and reduced without resorting to the methods of traditional measurement-based evaluation.

IDENTIFYING A SET OF TRUSTWORTHY AND CREDIBLE PROCEDURES

Reputable scientists who work in fields like anthropology, ethnography, sociology, and program evaluation have identified a range of procedures which they argue can be applied to data in order to ensure that research findings are 'trustworthy' (reliable) and 'credible' (valid). These procedures have technical names which might be off-putting at first glance. However, the concepts that these labels represent are really quite logical and as one of our co-researchers commented, 'very commonsensical'. Many of them are things that teachers are already doing, but are not aware of. It is our belief that when teachers are consciously aware of what they are, how they work together, and why they need to be consciously used, they become empowered evaluators.

These procedures are:

- prolonged engagement on the site (being there)
- persistent observation (observing until you know what's salient)
- triangulation (crosschecking)
- peer debriefing (having a peer keep you honest)
- negative case analysis (consciously looking for examples that could disprove your emerging interpretations)
- referential adequacy (keeping lots of products or 'references' that confirm your interpretations)
- member checking (taking your interpretations back to the members of the 'tribe' and asking them to tell you whether they agree with them)

Prolonged engagement on the site

This procedure simply means what it says. It means being there long enough to build up trust and to understand the culture well enough to be able to make sense of what takes place.

Classroom teachers, by the very nature of their job, can't help applying this procedure. On average they spend about six hours a day, five days per week, for about forty weeks of the year in a culture we call 'the classroom'. There are few who would argue that this procedure cannot or is not being applied. It's a by-product of the job.

Persistent observation

This procedure complements prolonged engagement. If prolonged engagement at the site means being a part of the culture, persistent observation serves to identify what is salient in that culture, what is worth paying close attention to.

If teachers are to identify the range of markers of learning they can use to evaluate learning, they must persistently observe, in a focused way, what goes on in classrooms. Only through persistent observation can they hope to identify, recognise and make use of the markers of learning. Our data show that teachers need to make explicit their values and beliefs about literacy before they can begin to identify what markers or indicators of student growth they can use. Persistent observation is what makes this possible.

Triangulation

This is yet another way of improving the credibility of findings. The term is a geometrical metaphor based on the practice of identifying the source of a radio broadcast by using directional antennae set up at two ends of a known baseline. By measuring the angle at which each of the antennae receive the strongest signal the source can be pinpointed using simple geometry.

When applied to assessment and evaluation at the classroom level it simply means 'crosschecking by using multiple and different sources of data about the same literacy behavior'.

Peer debriefing

Peer debriefing is a little different from the three previous procedures. It provides an external check on what is collected and interpreted. It involves finding a peer who has no vested or emotional interest in the students you're evaluating, and sharing your methods and your findings in ways that enable you to be 'kept honest'. It is important that this peer be one who knows and understands teaching in ways that you do. This peer typically plays the role of devil's advocate, asking searching questions and forcing you to make explicit and examine your biases and prejudices, and constantly suggesting alternative interpretations of your information which you have to refute and/or accept.

While this may not currently be a regular part of your assessment and evaluation practice, it is one that should not be too hard to implement in schools. An example would be a grade meeting at which all the Year 3 teachers met and discussed their interpretations of different students' learning growth (or lack thereof), and justified for their peers how and why they came to the conclusions they reached. Another would be an informal meeting over lunch in which you ask another teacher to listen to your interpretations and comment on them as a fellow professional.

Negative case analysis

This procedure helps ensure that we don't get too carried away by first impressions, or by any unconscious biases we might have. If, for example, we unconsciously believe that boys will always perform better at maths (or science, reading, writing, etc.) than girls, we may collect information about the boys and girls in our class that tends to support this belief. Thus we may keep ranking the top boy mathematician (scientist, reader, etc.) in our class above the top girl, and may even argue that we have the data to prove it.

But what if on some occasions we actually observe this girl helping explain difficult concepts to the top boy who, without this help, obviously wouldn't have been able to perform as well on the other criteria you typically use? This is one example of behavior which negates our first impression. That is, it's a negative case. We should use it to rethink and reassess our belief that the boy really is perhaps NOT a better mathematician. In responsive evaluation we need to be consciously looking for negative cases that will cause us to rethink and re-examine the conclusions we begin to form about different learners.

The more of these we can call upon to show that we have been alert to alternative conclusions, the more credible and trustworthy our findings will be.

Referential adequacy

This simply refers to written records (or other records such as TV/audio tapes) which can be used both to illustrate and support interpretations and conclusions that emerge from other sources of information.

The most familiar example of this procedure currently in use in literacy classrooms is the recent move to 'folders' or 'portfolios' of student products which are used to evaluate learning. While most classrooms use a sample of student written products to include in such portfolios, there are some classrooms which capture student literacy behaviors on video and/or audiotape and include these as a source of information to interpret and report.

We came to the conclusion that if the assessment and evaluation procedure we have operating in our classrooms are described as being referentially adequate, this simply means we have a rich and varied source of written and/or other documentary materials to support our findings.

Member checking

Member checking refers to the practice of taking the information you interpret back to the members of stakeholding groups. In most classrooms this would mean taking your evaluations of student learning back to the students themselves and asking them to comment on your findings and conclusions. It could also involve doing the same thing with others who have a stake in the conclusions you draw about the learner, especially parents, and perhaps other teachers and administrators. It can be done both formally and informally.

Teachers who continually share with students the reasons behind the judgements they make about their learning, and who authentically listen to and respond to their complaints or confusions are informally carrying out a continual form of member checking. The process of constant member checking complements the other procedures in terms of reducing threats to fairness and equity.

WHAT'S THE RESULT OF CONSCIOUSLY APPLYING THESE PROCEDURES?

When these procedures are consciously applied by teachers in the daily ebb and flow of their classrooms our findings indicate that they become very confident about the conclusions they are able to draw about each of their students. This confidence is increased when they can show parents, peers, and administrators to whom they're accountable, the trail of evidence they have used to arrive at the conclusions they draw. This trail, sometimes referred to as an 'audit trail' can be a very convincing demonstration of the credibility (validity in traditional language) of what they find out about each student's learning.

When Dianne was asked how all that we've just described helped her, she replied:

First it helped me understand how responsive evaluation could be as rigorous and valid, (i.e. 'trustworthy and credible') as more traditional measurement-based approaches.

Second it helped me get control of the language I needed in order to talk about and justify what I was doing in the name of evaluation.

CONCLUSION

While many teachers may once have felt helpless and powerless in the face of criticisms that claimed that qualitative approaches to assessment and evaluation were 'soft' and/or 'subjective' and therefore 'unscientific', our findings show that when they begin to implement the credibility procedures described above, when they begin to get control of the language which is used to describe and discuss these procedures they feel confident and secure about defending and justifying their decision to implement responsive evaluation.

Furthermore, when faced with mandated policies that insist on a measurement-based approach to assessment and evaluation, our findings also show that they begin to understand how they can make use of the information provided by standardised tests as simply one more piece of information in the 'big picture' of each of their students' learning growth. What is more important is that all reported a sense of empowerment that made teaching a more enjoyable and satisfying experience, and that this sense of enjoyment and satisfaction spilled over to their students and ultimately the parents.

References

Anthony, R.J., Johnson, T.D., Mickelson, N.I. and Preece, A. 1991. *Evaluating Literacy: A Perspective for Change*, Portsmouth, NH: Heinemann.

Barth, R. 1991. *Improving Schools from Within*. San Francisco, CA: Jossey-Bass.

Betts, F. 1992. "How Systems Thinking Applies to Education." *Educational Leadership*, 50(3): 38–44.

Brandt, R. 1989. "On Misuse of Testing: A Conversation with George Madaus." *Educational Leadership*, 47(7): 26–9.

Brown, H. and V. Mathie. 1991. *Inside Whole Language*. Rozelle: Primary English Teaching Association; Portsmouth, NH: Heinemann.

Brown, R. 1991. *Schools of Thought*. San Francisco, CA: Jossey-Bass.

Cambourne, B.L. 1988a. *Directions in Language Learning: The Push for Accountability Testing*. Paper presented at the South Coast Region's Conference, Moss Vale, N.S.W.

———. 1988b. *The Whole Story*. Auckland: Ashton Scholastic.

Cambourne, B.L. and J. Turbill. 1990. "Assessment in Whole Language Classrooms: Theory into Practice." *The Elementary School Journal*, 90(3): 337–49.

Cordeiro, P. 1992. *Whole Language and Content in the Upper Elementary Grades,* New York: Richard Owens.

Costa, A. 1989. "Re-assessing Assessment." *Educational Leadership*, 46:7.

Cuttance, P. 1994. *The Development of Quality Assurance Reviews in the NSW School System: What Works?* Sydney: NSW Department of School Education, Quality Assurance Directorate.

Fullan, M. 1990. "Staff Development, Innovation, and Instructional Development." In *Changing School Culture Through Staff Development*, edited by B. Joyce. Alexandria, VA: Association for Supervision and Curriculum Development.

Fullan, M. and A. Hargreaves. 1991. *Working Together for Your School*. Auburn: ACEA.

Guba, E.G., and Y.S. Lincoln. 1981. *Effective Evaluation*. San Francisco, CA: Jossey-Bass.

———. 1989. *Fourth Generation Evaluation*. Newbury Park, CA: Sage.

Hancock, J. 1991. The Descriptive Analysis and Evaluation of the Process Experienced by a Teacher Researcher in Implementing Responsive Evaluation as a Model of Assessment of Literacy Development in a Whole Language Classroom. Unpublished M.Ed. Thesis, University of Wollongong.

Holdaway, R.D. 1974. *The Foundations of Literacy*. Auckland: Ashton Scholastic; 1979, Portsmouth, NH: Heinemann.

Krashen, S.D. and T.D. Terrell. 1988. *The Natural Approach: Language Acquisition in the*

Classroom, Oxford: Pergamon; Eaglewood Cliffe, NJ: Alemany Press

Lincoln, Y.S. and Guber, E. 1985. *Naturalistic Inquiry*. Beverly Hills, CA: Sage.

NSW Department Of School Education, 1994. *English K-6 Syllabus*.

Pearson, D. and S. Valencia. 1987. "Assessment, Accountability, and Professional Prerogative." In *Research in Literacy: Merging Perspectives*. Thirty-sixth Yearbook of the National Reading Conference (pp. 3–15).

Peshkin, A. 1988. "In Search of Subjectivity: One's Own." *Educational Researcher*, 17(7): 17–21.

Resnick, L.B. 1987. "Learning in and out of School", *Educational Researcher*, 16(9), pp. 13-20.

Rorty, R. 1991. *Objectivity, Relativism, and Truth: Philosophical Papers*. Volume 1, Sydney: Cambridge University Press; (1990) New York, NY; Cambridge University Press.

Schwandt, T. 1989. "Solutions to the Paradigm Conflict: Coping with Uncertainty." *Journal of Contemporary Ethnography*, 17(4): 379–407.

Shepard, L. 1989. "Why We Need Better Assessments." *Educational Leadership*, 46(7), pp. 4-9

Stake, R. 1975. *Evaluating the Arts in Education: A Responsive Approach*. Columbus, OH: Merrill.

Turbill, J., A. Butler, and B. Cambourne. 1991. *Frameworks*. New York: Wayne-Finger Lakes Board of Co-operative Educational Services.

Watson, D. 1989. "Defining and Describing Whole Language." *The Elementary School Journal*, 90(2): 129–141.

Woodward, H.L. 1992. *Negotiated Evaluation*. Rozelle: Primary English Teaching Association; 1994, Portsmouth, NH: Heinemann.

Index